Hey _____, Here's Your Present...

IT'S A BOOK!

Robert
Beiderman

---

decorations by Michael Wetstone

CONTENTS

Introduction.................................... 1

Why did I get this book?......................... 3

What can I do with this book?.................... 23

What else can I do with this book?............... 47

What <u>can't</u> I do with this book? 63

What type of book is this?....................... 75

What did I do to deserve this book?.............. 99

How can this book help me pick up women
(or men)?....................................... 119

What other gifts would I have received,
if not for this book?........................... 135

How can I re-gift this book? 149

To the amazing Mr. Wetstone,

Your wonderful sketches lift my dreams to new heights...

May your next vegan cheeseburger be filled with substantial flavor (and Lord knows what else).

Introduction

    Congratulations! You are the proud owner of a brand new book! Or perhaps a used one. Hey, you've got a book. That's pretty cool. Did you know that in parts of the entire state of New Jersey, a book is considered a rather large status symbol? Neither did I... But it must be true, because one of us just read it. So make sure to thank your friend / husband / wife / daughter / son / cousin / aunt / uncle / brother / sister / co-worker / dominatrix / employee trying to suck up / guilt-ridden scumbag who was sleeping with your wife / dentist / stalker / friend of a friend who didn't even want to come to your party in the first place for this amazing birthday / holiday / wedding / get well soon / sorry I slept with your wife present that you will certainly cherish for the rest of your life.

    You probably have many questions about how to make this the best gift ever. Rest assured, the following chapters will guide you to getting the most out of this book. We'll cover everything this tome can do for you, from holding your sandwich to taking your mind off that diet to making your car more valuable to showing people that you don't know karate... this manuscript was specifically written for <u>you</u>. Every page was written with those beautiful blue / brown / hazel / zombie red eyes engraved into my brain, remembering how much I love to stare at that blonde / brown / black / red hair on your head / balls. So let's not waste another minute here. Let's get to reading! Going to watch television? Catch it in repeats. Going to the movies? Catch it on Blu-Ray. Going to see U2 in concert? There'll be another one next year. Seriously, when Bono sings "I still haven't found what I'm looking for," I think he's referring to a city that he hasn't already performed in. They get around more than Perez Hilton at a webcam convention. Going to have sex with your wife? Just place this book above her head. Going to have sex with your husband? He won't mind. Plus, it will probably be over soon, anyway.

      Now before you fully embrace your good fortune, you may want to take a moment and give thanks to your religious deity, or to science, or to Lady Gaga… whichever you believe in the most. It is also recommended that you make plans to give back to your local charity, as a way of truly earning this life-changing experience. Might I recommend the National Audubon Society? Most people think they're for the birds. You should also amend your will in the near future; otherwise this book could fall into the wrong hands after you walk by that pizza shop on Main Street at 1:42 in the afternoon on November 7th, 2023. Finally, turn your phone off and find yourself a comfy chair. You have a book to read! Take a deep breath… and enjoy!

Why did I get this book?

You might find yourself asking how you could be so blessed, as to receive this wonderful book today. Don't be alarmed. That's perfectly normal. After all, there are so many other — less impressive — gifts you could have received. Be grateful the fates were smiling upon you... but if you really must examine this issue, we'll delve into some of the factors that probably came into play to enrich your life for the better:

• **Somebody cares about you.** See? You're not a total jerk! Perhaps you have been a little grumpy lately, but at least one person has chosen to see through that gruff exterior to understand that wasn't the real you acting like a total bitch. Maybe you haven't been keeping up with your share of the chores, or paying alimony on time. Maybe you borrowed the car and forgot to fill it up with gas before returning it, only you were too preoccupied with the stranger you ran over because you were doing 80 mph in a school zone while hopped up on amphetamines. Look, we're all human. We make mistakes from time to time. Thankfully for you, one person likes you and accepts you for who you truly are. They know you deserve the very best, and by golly you've got it!

- **You have enough coffee mugs.** Who in this world does not have enough coffee mugs? You have that set of mugs that was given to you as a gift when you moved into your new home. You have that set of mugs that you bought on sale, when all you were shopping for was a new pillow case after one of your uncontrollable "drooling" incidents. You have that mug you stole from the office, because nobody else in accounting appreciated the irony of the cartoon on the side as you did. You have that mug for being the world's greatest husband / wife / boss / grandparent / brother / dog / warden / one-night stand / designated driver / lobbyist / stunt double / coffee maker. You have that mug which reminds you to cheer up, and that mug that reminds you how special you are.

You even have that mug that reminds you how you'll never be as successful as your older brother / sister... although I have no idea why you still keep that one in the house. Enough already! If you get one more coffee mug you're probably going to slit your wrists with a broken piece of cheap ceramic made in China. This is the dawning of a new day. Suck it, coffee mug industry! You've made a fortune off the stupid impulses of our nation long enough.

- **Somebody knows that you can read.** You thought it was your little secret. Just play dumb and stare blankly during office presentations. Squint your eyes and look confused when news bulletins scroll by on the bottom of the television screen. But then one day you passed by a copy of *Us Weekly* with Jennifer Aniston and Angelina Jolie on the cover. And you just couldn't resist taking a peek, could you? Did Jennifer forgive Angelina? Was Jennifer secretly pregnant with Brad's baby? Did Angelina adopt an alien from the planet Uranus? My gosh, it could be ANYTHING! Five minutes later you had been caught red-handed. Sure, you tried to pretend that you were just staring at the pictures, but deep down you knew the truth. Everybody knew. Word spreads fast, and from that day on you became known as someone who reads. It was only a matter of time before the dots could be connected, and your journey would lead you down the path to this day... and this book.

- **With the decline in new home building, there were some extra trees available.** People haven't been buying new homes for years now, but that's no reason to stop cutting down trees. After all, there are like… thousands of trees out there just taking up space. If we don't use these trees the woodpeckers will, and then the woodpeckers will win, and then we'll have to listen to that stupid woodpecker laugh for the rest of our lives. It was hard enough putting up with that laugh just on Saturday mornings. So what else can we use trees for? Some might suggest fire wood, but thanks to global warming we don't need much of that now, either. And pirate ships have switched to fiberglass over the years. (Hey, at least you don't get splinters when you walk the plank now.) The best use for dead trees is still paper. Now with newspapers going the way of dinosaurs, cassette players and Wilmer Valderrama's career, the best use of paper is for books. Lots of books. Books that make great gifts.

- **The person who bought you this book is probably a friend of the author.** You might want to check with the person who gave you this and see if we have ever met. Trust me, I have pestered the living #^*! out of everyone I know to buy a million copies. People I haven't seen in 20 years, who thought I had erased their contact information, were wrong. If they're on Facebook, Myspace, Twitter, Linkden, Friendster or the Sex Offender website, I've found them… which makes you a very lucky individual.

Do you know someone who once lived / worked / visited / was arrested in New York, New Jersey, California, Massachusetts, Florida, Texas, Nevada, Ohio, Pennsylvania, Arizona, Michigan, Wisconsin, Minnesota, Illinois, Kentucky or Europe? If so, they might have met me. We might have shared a laugh about the weather or competed against each other in an underground demolition derby tournament. Perhaps we accidentally dated the same woman or woke up in the same back alley one morning. Either way, the two of us became good friends. And I eventually hunted that friend down and pestered... uh, persuaded them into buying this book, which you now own. You're welcome.

• **You're a hard person to shop for.** You're allergic to chocolate. You wear size extra-medium. You can't stand Kevin Bacon. And we all know that any cash you receive is immediately being converted into Bitcoin. Face it, you're impossible to shop for. It's gotten to the point where you don't even bother to fake a smile when you open your presents. Family members have started to just hand you the gift receipt and leave your actual gift in the car... with the engine running. When they once donated a gift to charity in your name, you actually called the charity to have your name removed from it. Even those surprise tickets to Cancun went to waste when a certain somebody forgot to renew your passport. Good thing we've finally found something you can use and appreciate.

• **Any day can be a holiday.** Now that you've received the best present on Earth, you'll want to pay it forward to the rest of your loved ones. Thankfully, the best holidays don't always take place at the end of December. There are actually many opportunities each month to give someone a gift, and a book is the perfect gift for most of these occasions. Think I'm kidding? You really do need to be more trusting. Here are a few holidays that can best be celebrated with a good book:

> o **February:** When's the last time you gave your wife / girlfriend / child's babysitter / third cousin the rest of the family has yet to learn about a book for **Valentine's Day (2/14)**?

Let's think about this for just a minute. Even if your belle is not allergic to flowers, they're sure to be disappointed when the flowers die after only a few days. Chocolates will only make them gain weight and fill them with self-loathing; good luck trying to get some action after that sets in. And jewelry... you'll probably want to save this for when you really need to make amends after you say something ill-advised around her, like pretty much anything. By giving your woman a book, you are handing her a lifetime of knowledge. Knowledge is power. Power is equality. Equality brings peace. And peace brings a good night's sleep.

Now ladies, your husband / boyfriend / prison pen pal / son's best friend / college professor will always appreciate a good book, because you can only read *Popular Mechanic* on the can so many times. But even with this loving gift for him, you'll probably still have to put out.

o **March:** This is the month that enters like a lion and leaves like a lamb. And just as a mother lion protects her cubs, you'll want to stock up on mascara and sensible shoes to celebrate **International Women's Day (3/8)**. Women have come a long way since they were being burned at the stake. Now they serve in the army, on the Supreme Court and at Red Lobster. They run corporations and drive racecars... all while wearing high heels. Kelly Kulick beat 30 men to win the 2010 Professional Bowling Association's Tournament of Champions. And their leader, Oprah, is more powerful than any man on earth. Speaking of Oprah... do you know how to get on her good side? Through her book club! Women are all about reading. So get that special woman in your life a book, and if you fellows want to get back to the top of that mountain someday... perhaps you need to read a few more books yourselves.

o **April:** You don't have to live in America to appreciate a wonderful book. Keeping with the international theme, April brings us **World Book & Copyright Day (4/23)**. Every year the United Nations celebrates this holiday by distributing a poster of the world with an open book in it. I'm excited already! This date also marks the death of William Shakespeare and a bunch of other writers you've probably never heard of. These people spent their entire lives writing for your enjoyment and helped the people who own Cliffnotes eventually earn a lot of money. It would be an insult not to open a book on this day. And you do not want to insult people from other countries. I believe that World War I began after Archduke Ferdinand refused to join Gavrilo Princip's book club. With our country's unwillingness to embrace soccer or go without deodorant, reading books might be the only activity we can share with the rest of the world. So try reading a book… for peace.

o **May:** Now that spring is in bloom and it's safe to wear white again for a few months, we can let our hair down a little and celebrate **Rhode Island Independence Day (5/4)**. That's right, Rhode Island… you don't need to take crap from anyone! You read whatever you want to read. In fact, you can read your books stark naked in the middle of the White Horse Tavern if you want.

You're the Ocean State. Anyone who messes with you gets the full fury of the Atlantic. And since you're the size of my living room, I suggest the rest of the world read books in your honor. But don't get too crazy, becuae the following day is **Cinco de Mayo (5/5)**. I have no idea what this holiday stands for or why it takes place on the 5th of May every year, but I do know that people like to have a good time during it... and nothing is more fun than reading your favorite book. For those of your friends who accidentally celebrated the evening with Dos Equis instead of Dostoevsky, you should make sure to read to them (loudly) first thing the following morning... preferably over a plate of runny eggs and tunafish. You and your friends will have almost two full weeks to recover before the start of **World Information Society Day (5/17)**. This holiday was created by the United Nations in 2006 to celebrate the power of the internet and other communication technologies. Wait a minute.... What?! First of all, the internet is just a fad. It's only use is for showing people where they can buy books. Real books, made of paper, that you can hold in your hand. Thankfully, most countries stopped listening to the UN decades ago. So join us in telling the UN to shove their diplomatic crush on the internet, and get your information from an old-fashioned book.

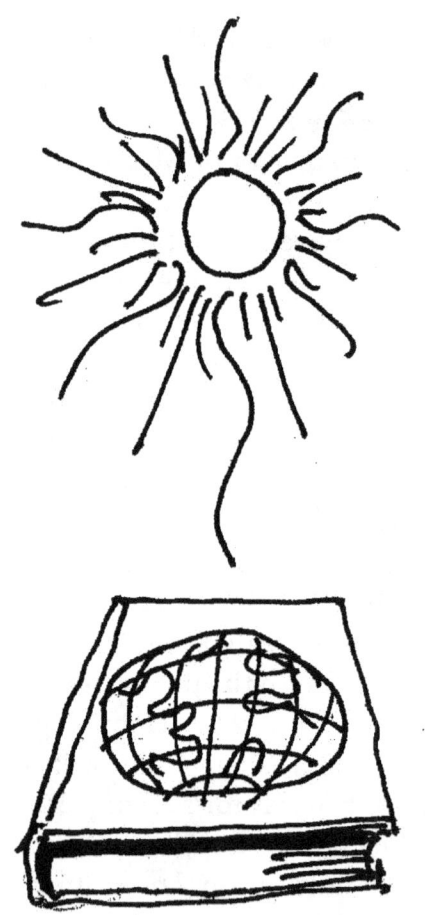

o **June:** They've been with you through thick and thin. They've seen you at your best and at your worst. They know all about that little "experiment" in college, your eating disorder and that hitchhiker you killed in Costa Rica. Basically, you don't want to piss him / her off. So make sure you show some love to the person who is always there for you on **National Best Friends Day (6/8)**. You know how much your best friend loves to read based on their diary, blogs, Facebook and Twitter pages, and confession note. And considering the number of texts that you Rocky and Bullwinkles like to send each other, I'll bet your buddy likes to read a lot, too. Worried that there's not enough time in the day to read a good book? That won't be a problem for you Northern Hemisphere folks during the **Summer Solstice (6/21)**. On this day light shines eternal; plenty of extra time to catch up on your favorite book!

o **July:** If there was ever a month designed to celebrate the invention of books, this is the one. First up, we pay homage to those lovable Canucks up north on **Canada Day (7/1)**. Whether you're ice-fishing, backpacking around the globe or mispronouncing vowels, Canadians make everything more enjoyable. So head over to the nearest Tim Hortons and give your northern neighbor a wonderful book, while hockey season is still a few months away. Only one day later, it's time to acknowledge those brave Americans who took the time to learn how to read, with **National Literacy Day (7/2)**. Great Americans and reading have been linked to each other dating all the way back to the founding fathers. Think about it. If the men who signed the Declaration of Independence didn't know how to read, Thomas Jefferson could have written anything. He could have stated that we want the right to worship squirrels, and the rest of the founders would have just gone along with it. Then we would all find ourselves knee-deep in acorns today, while still being forced to pay way too much for a decent cup of tea and listening constantly to One Direction. Next in our wise Cancer month is **Teddy Bear Picnic Day (7/10)**. Imagine you've driven an hour into the woods with your favorite stuffed bear, and found a nice clearing with a beautiful view of the lake. You set out your blanket and passed out the sandwiches and Shasta. It's been a pleasant afternoon, but it's only a matter of time before the conversation dries up. There are only so many times you can put up with this damn bear complaining about how hot it is under all that fur, or the time that you chewed on its ear. And don't forget that you still have a long drive home ahead of you.

So you're going to need a little entertainment. Good thing this book will provide you with discussion topics for you and your teddy bear, such as:

- Who's sexier: Yogi Bear or Winnie the Pooh?
- When will the Care Bears finally check into rehab?
- Why isn't Barbie eating more?
- Who put Mr. Potato Head in the Easy Bake Oven?
- How many lives does the family cat have left?

This holiday was actually named after a song that was written in the early 1900's. Don't listen to it. It's really creepy. You'll have nightmares. Good thing you sleep with a teddy bear to keep you safe at night.

Next we go from an animal stuffed with cotton to an animal sometimes stuffed with cheese, as we keep the love going with **Cow Appreciation Day (7/14)**. The exact date of this holiday changes from year to year, but I like the idea of having something else to celebrate on Bastille Day. Unlike the French, you'll never see a cow raising its hands in the air to surrender. Look, cows don't ask for much. So instead of tipping over a cow on this day, why not show some kindness and read to it from your favorite book. And maybe eat some chicken today. You can always wear leather chaps and eat a cheeseburger tomorrow. Finally, you'll want to make sure to have a good book at the ready for **Rain Day (7/29)**, celebrated in Waynesburg, PA, where it rains 90% of the time on this date. Hey, with the right book any day can be a rain day!

o **August:** As summer comes to a close, you deserve a break. Take your phone off the hook, grab a cold beverage from the fridge and relax with a good book for **Lazy Day (8/10)**. My suggestion is to read a chapter, take a nap, read a chapter, take a nap, stretch and repeat. You can skip the stretching if you feel that's too much work. I tried asking an expert in laziness how this holiday is celebrated; he never returned my call. Now when you finally do resume work,

make sure to you give yourself a hand... literally. Only one is needed to celebrate **International Lefthanders Day (8/13)**. This holiday was probably created by the New York Mets' front office, because they're never right. Most of you know that the left side of your brain is more logical and rational, while the right side of your brain is more intuitive and subjective. And that the right side of your brain is actually connected to your left hand. So this means that lefthanders are more likely to be intuitive. Hence, they like to read. This will all make sense to you, if you're right-handed.

o **September:** So you missed out on National Literacy Day back in July. You're not alone. Would you believe the rest of the world missed it, too? From the invention of blue jeans to the Big Mac, America just seems to be out in front of the pack. Now would be a good time to brush up on your foreign accents with **International Literacy Day (9/8)**. Apparently other countries took a good look at us and figured that if the people of Alabama could read, so could they. Either way, you should do a lot of reading this day to prove to everyone that Uncle Sam still has what it takes. From an uncle to older relatives, you'll want to cherish **National Grandparents Day (9/13)**. Forget the fact that they're ugly and smell weird. Without your grandparents, you would never have been born. They deserve something really special. So what do old people like? Well, they're not a big fan of technology. They probably have no idea how to work a computer and think a "blu ray" is some form of jazz. And they already have enough hard candies to last a lifetime... well, their lifetime... which won't be very long. When your grandparents were young, the only form of entertainment they knew was reading, by candlelight. So give them something they'll understand, like a good old-fashioned book. Just don't buy them one that has too many pages. Remember, these people don't even buy green bananas anymore.

o **October:** Only a few weeks before we dress up like sexy vampires and beg strangers for candy, we celebrate **World Mental Health Day (10/10)**. This is especially needed in years where Michael Bay has released more than zero films. Reading is the best exercise for your brain, especially if you read it backwards. So take a day off from reruns of *Dawson's Creek*, and stimulate your mind with a clever book. Besides, statistics show that KFC and donuts have probably done a number on the rest of your body. Mental health is likely the only thing you have left. Traveling across the pond towards the end of this month? You won't want to be caught unprepared for **National Tell a Story Day (10/27)** in the United Kingdom. Don't worry if you have less stories to tell than a monk in a coma. There are plenty of great tales in a book. From Hercules to Harry Potter to Heidi Fleiss' memoir, books have been a great source of fiction for centuries. This tome provides plenty of exciting anecdotes to share with the Brits over a pint of ale and a plate of your favorite starch. Just steer clear from that story of George Washington and his army crossing the Delaware River. I hear they're still a little sore over the ending of that one.

o **November:** In honor of this last holiday, your manuscript is chopping off 70% from its usual wit. On the last Friday of this month comes perhaps the craziest holiday of them all, **Black Friday**. It's nearly impossible to focus on buying a book when there are iPads on sale for under $100, so you'll want to get one ahead of this holiday for the poor folks who spend all night camping out for these sales. It must get pretty boring just sitting in that sleeping bag / tent / blanket / Ford Fiesta in a vacant Wal-Mart parking lot. If only they had something to keep them company, to entertain them. Unlike a monkey with an accordion, this book won't make you go deaf or throw its feces at anyone. They'll be able to relax among the 200 other crazies before the big day, which is something that everyone can truly be thankful for... 364 days from now.

What can I do with this book?

Books aren't just for reading. Although if you do find yourself in a situation that calls for reading, I suppose you could do a lot worse than a book. Whether you're looking to cure boredom or syphilis, everything you need is in this book. Consider it the Swiss army knife of literature. It will provide you with knowledge, diversions, props and alibis. (Where were you the night that forest fire was started near your camp site? You were with this book, officer! Case closed.) So buckle up and free your mind to the many wonders of your brand new book. Here is just a sampling of the ways it will enrich you:

• **Survive rush hour.** Isn't it amazing how a simple 20 mile trip can take three hours? Your car-pool buddy might be able to sleep in the passenger seat, but unfortunately you need to be somewhat awake. Unlike the radio, you'll find that this book is commercial free. And while that *Cinderella* DVD looks tempting, the stupid car manufacturer forgot to put a monitor near the driver's seat. Let yourself get lost in the printed word, and you might even find yourself looking forward to this commute. And don't worry about knowing when it's time to drive. The cars behind you will be sure to let you know when traffic has finally started moving again.

- **Outlast travel delays.** There's nothing more frustrating than when you experience delays on your way to your vacation / client meeting / lovers' rendezvous / bank robbery / Teen Choice Awards. But they do happen from time to time, especially on American Airlines. The best thing you can do is try to take your mind off the excruciating wait. Sometimes this is easier said than done. After all, there's really nothing good to look at.... except for maybe that blonde three rows in front of you, and her boyfriend is really, REALLY huge. Don't risk it, bro. I wouldn't recommend trying to have a conversation with the person sitting next to you, because he's probably busy trying to conceal illegal pills up his butt, anyway. And save the battery on your iPhone. Your best option is to find something to read for the time being. How many times can you try to memorize the menu in the train's snack car, or look through that Sky Mall magazine on the plane without being brainwashed into buying the Pool Blaster Aqua Broom ($79.99)? You don't even own a pool! Trust me, you're much better off with a good book. Hey, look at that... you're already moving! Oh... you're not? Hang in there; I'm sure you will be soon. And just in case, there's still plenty of book here for you to read.

- **Protect yourself from sick passengers.** Whether you are traveling by plane, train, car or boat, motion sickness can strike anyone at any time. A real man holds down his or her lunch, but you can't always count on being seated next to a real man. So if the chicken cacciatore and Bud Lights your neighbor ate for lunch come back up for an encore, you're going to need protection in a hurry. Good thing this trusty barf-repellant book is already in your hands. As soon as you see those cheeks fill up like a hibernating chipmunk, put the book up to your face and look in the other direction. Don't be squeamish. It will all be over soon. And don't show too much compassion when he / she is apologizing afterwards. The laws of our land dictate that any food particles which remain stuck to this book are yours to keep.

- **Smack the kid who is kicking your seat.** Traveling in itself will make a person tense, and that brat sitting behind you isn't helping matters. The repeated kicking motion to your lower back isn't having the massaging effect you would hope for. Politely asking the little terror to stop kicking you went in one headphone-covered ear and out the other, and lord knows the parent busy playing *Angry Birds* is oblivious to your plight. What courteous measures have failed to accomplish, a swift smack to the head will achieve. Now, it's illegal to hit a child with your fist, so stay out of trouble and use this book. Don't worry about it hurting too much. After all, this is "light" reading material.

- **Ignore pan-handlers on the subway.** After working a long day at the office / restaurant / fire station/ light bulb factory / funnel cake kiosk / White House, all you want to do is get home in one piece. Your subway ride is going smoothly until the stop before yours, when somebody on your car starts making a speech / singing a song / doing a dance / holding a hand-written sign in a non-verbally loud manner about being homeless / broke / deaf / blind / crippled / gay / straight / mute. As they make their way down the car in your direction, you realize that you will be forced to deal with this distraction before you reach your destination. It's at that moment you can pull out your favorite book, and instantly become so engrossed that you fail to notice this person standing two inches in front of you with a hand out. This book is so enthralling, it will actually make you blind, deaf <u>and</u> mute to the pan-handler in front of you for the immediate future. After a couple of seconds the beggar will move on to the next individual, and this book will have just saved you 25 cents. Over the next six months, it will practically pay for itself!

- **Shield your eyes from the sun.** It's a beautiful summer day. The grass is green, the flowers are in bloom and your hot neighbor is practically naked while getting a tan. Too bad you can't see any of it, because that pesky sun is shining right into your eyes. Neither sunglasses nor a wicker hat are anywhere in reach, and

you have really tiny hands. Fortunately, your book is more than capable of providing shade while you read. Just make sure that the outside of the book is facing the sun, while the inside is facing your eyes... unless you really enjoy staring at the cover. Time will fly as you relish your reading activity and peek around the edge of this book to keep tabs on that hot neighbor. You can fix those strange tan-lines on the rest of your face at a later date.

- **Shield yourself from a flying rubber band.** You are never safe. Flying objects can and will appear out of nowhere. Wherever there are people or orangutans with a vicious sense of humor, your safety could be at risk. Imagine you are having a peaceful day, enjoying your favorite type of sandwich and a Fresca, when all of a sudden a rubber band comes flying out of nowhere and hits you right in the eyeball! People don't recover from these types of serious injuries. You'll spend the rest of your life wearing a pirate eye-patch, pretending you have scurvy to avoid the snickers of cruel neighborhood kids. If only you could have blocked that projectile before impact. Forget about using your hand. First of all, the rubber band could slip between the fingers. Second, the force of the rubber band striking your hand will create a welt. Then when you go to that job interview the next day, the pain will convince you not to shake the hand of your prospective boss, and this will not make a good first impression. "Who doesn't shake hands these days?" they will think. You won't get the job and will be stuck living with your parents for the next decade. Better to just use this book. It will keep you safe, and if you hold it at just the right angle you will ricochet that rubber band right back to the source from whence it came....
you guessed it, the orangutan.

- **Spoil the ending of Agatha Christie's *Murder on the Orient Express*.** They all killed him. Each of the 12 passengers stabbed him once, so that nobody could know which one delivered the fatal blow. I'm sorry, were you planning on reading that soon? I guess you didn't have any free time over the past 60 years. You should really thank me. I just saved you from reading over 300 pages of an inferior manuscript, which gives you even more time to enjoy this one. While we're at it, Sophie is a descendant of Jesus and Mary Magdalene, Holden winds up at a mental hospital and the whale wins.

- **Throw it at a mugger.** He's getting away! Some thug just swiped that old lady's purse and is now running for safety. You'll never catch him, thanks to that knee injury you suffered when you challenged Channing Tatum to a dance-off. Your best bet is to throw something at him and knock him off balance. Your watch is a bad idea; he'll just keep it and add that to his bounty. Chances are that your handkerchief won't travel the required distance. And your shoe became disqualified when some "genius" decided it was necessary to double-knot the laces this morning. Instead, try throwing this book in the mugger's direction. Even if it doesn't hit him, the mugger is sure to pick it up and read a couple of pages. This will give people who are more athletic than you the necessary time to catch up to him and make the arrest.

• **Have an excuse for a bad hair day.** It's the night of the big dance and your hair is a mess. Nobody will care about that spectacular dress / tuxedo / pant suit, when your hair looks like you were conducting electricity experiments. You need an explanation and you need one fast. This is where your book can help. Simply tell everyone that you were trying to get some beauty sleep before the dance, and you mistook this book for a comfy pillow. To make matters worse, some strands of hair accidentally slipped inside the book! When you woke up, those strands of hair were yanked out of place… making your hair look like the mismatched child of Kevin Spacey and Weird Al Yankovic. See? Now nobody will know about that discount hair stylist you went to. It was all your book's fault. Stupid book.

- **Help with spying on someone.** There she is... walking through the park to her office. Or maybe going to a dermatologist appointment. Or perhaps heading out for a tryst with her lesbian lover. You may not know all of the details yet, but you're going to find out. She'll never know you're watching her, as long as this inconspicuous book is covering your face. Just calmly flip through the pages as she walks right into your trap. This is the official book of private investigators and stalkers everywhere, although a court order states that you can't bring it within 1,000 feet of Charlize Theron. Feel free to jot down notes of your target's activities in the margins of this page. A baseball cap, fake mustache and sunglasses would probably help, too. Bail money is not included.

- **Pretend you're not being asked out.** Ugh! There's that guy who chatted with you for 15 minutes in the parking lot after the AA meeting. You pretended to care about his taxidermy collection and now he thinks the two of you are in love. He's sauntering towards you with a million dollar smile and a ketchup stain on his shirt. (Dear Lord, you hope that's a ketchup stain.) There's no time to find your phone in that oversized purse you carry with you, and you pulled the emergency appendectomy routine with the last guy... you can only go to the well so many times before the local hospital grows unappreciative of your tactics. Just bury your head in this book and you'll never hear him ask you out to Applebee's.

- **Make your car more valuable.** No matter how fancy your car is, you can always use a little more substance. Whether you drive a Mercedes or a Mazda, that car is eventually going to lose value, right? Not so fast! You can still increase its net worth by upgrading your accessories. Fancy rims and wiper blades that work can be quite expensive. Tinted windows are illegal in some states... generally the ones that get the most sun; go figure. One accessory that's certainly legal in every state (except South Carolina) is this book. It may only increase your car's monetary value by about 10 dollars, but the cultural value will be immeasurable.

- **Understand your drunk aunt's karaoke lyrics.** Your sweet uncle's wife has always thought of song lyrics as more of a suggestion than carved into stone. Throw in a glass of wine and four mojitos, and you'll have better luck understanding Bob Dylan before your tia at the microphone. Some of pop music's greatest hits are becoming all shook up, but this book can help you make some sense of it all:

  o **The B-52's "Love Shack"**
  Love Shack, baby's got back
  Baby, love dat
  Baby's got back in this love shack
  Radio shack, I need to buy batteries.....

o **Eminem's "The Monster"**
 I'm friends with the monster, I think it's dead
 Along with the whiskey inside of my head
 You can't cut me off, I come here all the time
 I want a Corona with a lemon.....

o **Gloria Gaynor's "I Will Survive"**
 Oh go it's my turn, I will survivor
 As long as I get on that show with Jeff Probt
 I've got all my drink to finish
 And my love for my liver... and onions.... mmmm.....

o **Rick Springfield's "Jessie's Girl"**
 I wish that I had Jessie's drink
 That looks good; is that a seabreeze?
 Where can I find a bartender to make that?
 Is that Jessy with a "Y" or a "J"......

o **Aretha Franklin's "Respect"**
 R-E-S-V-P-D-ME-B-MNOP
 Find my other shoe
 It's somewhere by the ladies room
 Socks are me, V-P-Z-T.....

o **Journey's "Don't Stop Believin'"**
 Don't stop zzzzzzzzzzzzzzzzzzzzzzzzzzz
 zzzzzzzzzzzzzzzzzzzzzzzzzzzzzzzzzzz
 Huh? Hold on to this glass
 I'm taking a leak; pause the song!

- **Check for gravity.** You ever have one of those dreams where you are floating though space? You pass Mars, the moons of Jupiter, a giant chocolate Easter bunny, the Milky Way nebulous and Andre Agassi. When you wake up suddenly (right after the Easter bunny has taken a bite out of you), it sometimes takes a few moments to realize that you are back home and safe on planet Earth. One way you can tell that you're still on Earth, is by checking for the presence of gravity. Earth has it; outer space does not. Hold your book in your hand and extend it away from your body. Try not to hold the book directly over your foot. If you must hold the book directly over your foot — due to balance issues or to punish that little piggy going to market — it is highly recommended that you wear steel toed shoes or at least hold an asprin in your free hand. Now let go of the book. If it falls to the ground, that means gravity is present and you are most likely on planet Earth... or you are being held captive on an alien space craft that has somehow learned to duplicate our atmosphere and they are probably about to commence a long series of invasive probes on you. Either way, it's all good.

- **Fan yourself or a stranger.** It's hotter outside than a jalapeno barbeque in the Sahara desert. Wearing that thermal underwear isn't helping, either. You really should check the weather before you leave the house. A little breeze sure would go a long way towards easing your suffering. Mother Nature isn't helping today, so it looks like you're on your own. To create a breeze, simply take your book and wave it back and forth. You will want to wave the book in your direction in order to actually feel the breeze that you are creating, unless you own a boomerang or a specially-equipped trampoline. Take note that the faster you move the book, the more wind you will create. Ah... doesn't that feel nice? You probably don't even notice the smell of your flesh burning anymore. Now, you might have noticed that the woman next to you is also hot. We should point out that this is more of a figurative *hot*, instead of the literal hot that you're experiencing. No matter... you should still offer to fan her with the book, too. Maybe it works, maybe it doesn't... but it's still much better than any of the awful pick-up lines you were probably going to use.

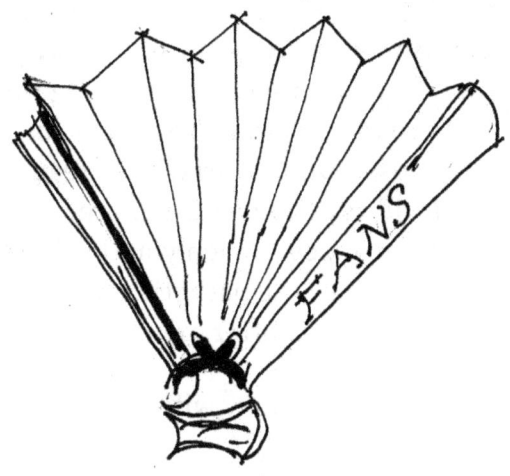

- **Hide that bloody nose.** Whether you're traveling to elevated heights or just digging for gold, you're occasionally going to strike red oil. It's only a matter of time before everyone around you notices that there is a stream of blood slowly trickling south across your face. Not everyone will buy the story you tell about your nose's menstrual cycle, so you better be prepared. This book can help buy you the valuable time that you need. Simply open the book to any page, and place it over your face. Angle the book in the direction that will shield you from the most people. With your free hand, you might want to cover your nostrils with a tissue or napkin. If the bleeding doesn't stop, throw your face into the nearest fist you can find. Then drop the book and start crying.

- **Read all of the things you've always wanted to say, but never had the guts to actually do it.**
You're a coward. I have no problem saying this to your face, because you're a coward. Are you crying already? Jeez… what a wuss! Don't worry, after reading these sentences you will start to feel like more of a man… or woman… or chimpanzee. When you think about it, anything is better than the pathetic excuse of a tadpole you are now. Just repeat after me:

o Stop sleeping with my wife.

o I'm canceling my gym membership.

o Yes, I am free this Saturday.
    No, I will not help you move.

o Yes, I am free this Saturday.
    No, I will not go out with you.

o Yes, I am free next Saturday.
    No, I will not go out with you then either.

o Yes, I am free most Saturdays.
    No, I will never go out with you, Uncle Albert.

o I'm buying the Porsche.

o Those jeans make you look fat.

- It's my birthday.
  We're having sex with the lights on.

- It's my birthday.
  We're watching *The Twilight Saga* again.

- It is not my birthday…
  But we're still going to Dave & Busters.

- If I had known there was no open bar, I would have bought a cheaper gift.

- If you didn't sign my paychecks, I would have stabbed you in the neck years ago.

- I voted for Walter Mondale.

- Of course she makes a tastier pound cake. Do you realize how much butter she uses in her lousy recipe? It's 1,000 calories! You're going to die.

- Meryl Streep is overrated.

- I don't care what the paternity test says. Your real father is Jack Daniels.

- *Avatar* was terrible, but I still masturbate to the blue alien.

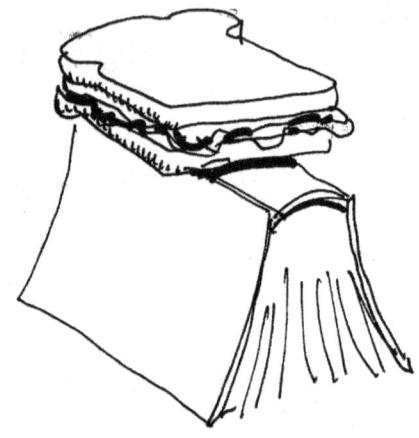

- **Hold your sandwich.** You are about to enjoy a scrumptious turkey and Swiss cheese sandwich on rye bread, with just a touch of Dijon mustard, when you realize that all of your plates are in the sink. Now is the time for eating, not cleaning or paying past-due rent. Good thing your book is just the right size for that tasty sandwich; after all, both are rectangular. You'll be pleasantly surprised at how this book provides a nice buffer between the table and your food. You can also transport your sandwich from one room to another on it. Remember, the more books you buy the more sandwiches you can hold! It can also transport a burrito, a slice of pizza, two potatoes, three bananas, and a cupcake. A scoop of ice-cream is not recommended.

- **Learn what it's like to read Hebrew.** Only 86% of adults in the United States know how to read, and that's just from left to right. Reading from right to left will make you a member of a much more exclusive tribe. Take the following sentence:

    o The frog jumped over the fence.

Warning: About 14% of you will not be able to read that… or this for that matter. For the rest of you, good job! Now, let's look at that sentence from above as the Hebrews would:

    o .ecnef eht revo depmuj gorf ehT

Mazel Tov! You are now reading like the Hebrews… only without all those squiggly, silly looking shapes and characters.

- **Stabilize a shaky table.** It's bad enough that your mother is kicking your butt in scrabble. She keeps inventing words, like "duenna" and "quark" and "mouthwash"... and for a triple-word score no less! You're down by 85 points, but you can still pull off an amazing comeback. Focus is the key right now, but your attention is being hijacked by this kitchen table that won't stop shaking. You've asked your mother if it would be okay to move this heated match into the living room, but your father is watching bowling highlights and doesn't want to be disturbed. If you don't stabilize that table soon, you'll go down in defeat and be forced to listen to your mother blab about your stupidity to all of her friends. Don't fret... here we come to the rescue! That's $R_1E_1S_1C_3U_1E_1$ = 8 pts. Take this book and slide it under the substandard table leg. If the book is too large (ie: full of too much knowledge), simply open and turn the pages until the table is stabilized. Now you'll be free to take Mom down and make her wish that you had put her in a nursing home.

- **Get fired from your job.** Sure, it's nice being able to pay your bills and feed yourself, but is this job really worth keeping? You were raised not to be a quitter, so it seems somebody will need to show you the door in order to taste freedom. Getting fired is easier said than done, since you always show up on time, do good work and are the boss' kid. Let's see if your new book can help you out. First, try reading this during a staff meeting. Make sure everyone notices you ignoring them, by flipping the pages as loudly as possible. If nobody says anything, start reading aloud and laughing. Cackle. Cackle like the wind. Still not getting a reaction? Throw the book at Steve in accounting. Make sure it hits him in the face. If that doesn't get you pulled into human resources, hit Steve again. Still not in trouble? Boy... they really don't like Steve in accounting. Perhaps you need to throw this book directly at someone in HR. If you still have a job after all of this insubordination, you might have to burn down the building. Luckily, this flammable book can help get that process started for you. However, you will need to buy a new book when all is said and done, presumably with your unemployment check.

- **Pretend you have a friend.** You've heard amazing things about that brand new Mexican / Italian / Sushi / BBQ / Fusion / Jamaican / Vegan / Burger King restaurant that opened across the street. For weeks you've wanted to try it for yourself, but nobody likes you. And we all know that you can't go by yourself. Good thing you have your book. Bring this along, and you'll be dining for two. Although you should be warned that your book did not bring a wallet in its jacket, so this round is on you.

• **Give yourself a headache, for the purpose of avoiding sex.** You've had a long day. You got caught in traffic on the way to work, then your car broke down, then it was broken into, and then set on fire. The coffee you drank was accidentally decaf, which you then spilled on your favorite pants. That boring staff meeting lasted forever. And you had to take the bus home, cook dinner and prepare for your fantasy football draft. The last thing you want to do now is have sex with your husband / wife / housekeeper / milkman / paparazzi / neighbor's pool boy / self. If only you had a headache! Simply take this book and whack yourself in the head as hard as you can. Repeat this motion as often as necessary, or until you black out. You can also try hitting yourself in the ear. This will add a helpful "ringing" sensation, and make it impossible for you to hear the desperate pleas of your disappointed partner.

What else can I do with this book?

You mean you're still not satisfied? Fine, there are plenty more amazing things that you can accomplish with the book that you're holding in your hands. It can bring you peace of mind and peace to the Middle East. Okay, one of those tasks might take longer than the other. So while we're working to solve Syria, try some of these:

• **Use it as a paperweight.** You're writing your annual letter to Santa Claus. After all, Santa might have a state-of-the-art workshop, thousands of unionized elves and the ability to know if every single person in the world has been naughty or nice... but he doesn't have email. After several drafts, you've almost found the perfect letter... the one that will certainly get you that toy ninja star you've long been craving. Too bad the breeze from that open window / ceiling fan / friendly Doberman wagging his tail / woman frantically waiving her hands in panic because her hair caught fire is blowing your previous drafts all over the room. To stabilize the situation, first gather all of the loose papers in your hand. Then place them on a flat surface and cover them with your book. Now you can get back to showing Santa how nice you've been this year. Feel free to enjoy a nice glass of eggnog while you write. Happy Holidays!

- **Look a little less pretentious in that café.** We get it. You're hip. It's a beautiful day outside, but you would rather spend your free time indoors surrounded by decaf chai cappuccinos. While most of the other Rachel Maddow lookalikes around you are buried in their laptops or discussing genetic food modification in South America, you can distance yourself from the truly pretentious by quietly reading this book in one of those oversized leather chairs next to the fake fireplace. You're just a regular Joe / Jane / Canadian who doesn't think you're better than anyone else... although the smoking pipe is probably a tad much.

- **Educate a stripper.** Sometimes taking off your clothes and shaking your booty for total strangers isn't very fulfilling. That is, for the stripper. Don't get me wrong; it's great for you, the customer. But for that poor fellow, the only thing that's well-rounded is his rear end. So grab a seat right next to the stage, where you can get a better view of his package than a UPS driver. While he's grooving in your general direction, open this book and start reading out loud to him. (You'll have to shout really loud to be heard over the music.) He'll be thrilled to hear from you. Knowledge is worth a lot more than a measly dollar. Besides, chances are that he's just doing this job to put himself through periodontal school anyway.

- **Take your mind off of that diet.** Good thing for you this book isn't edible, fatty. And there aren't any commercials for Jack in the Box or IHOP within these pages. It's just you and this book; no food allowed. Time will fly while you're having fun, without a single calorie added. In fact, you're bound to burn off some calories laughing at all of these witty jokes. Lose yourself in the pages of a good book, and your mind will be free of all those destructive temptations. There... all better. No desserts are on your mind. You've forgotten all about that cherry cheesecake with the fudge swirl that's sitting in your refrigerator... whoops!

- **Get sympathy.** Sometimes we just want a little TLC. Not the learning channel; watching television to learn is like using an enema to digest food... both will leave you hollow on the inside. We're talking about tender loving care. Most of us look pathetic enough on our own, but a few of you might need a little assistance in the pity department. Here are a few ways this book can help:

    o **Paper Cuts**: Take a single page of this book in your hands. Choose one of your fingers (try to avoid the middle one). Slide your finger quickly along the edge of the paper, slicing into the skin. Yell out in pain. Show your now injured finger to everyone around you. Post it on Facebook and Twitter. Skype it to a total stranger on the other side of the world. Everybody hates a paper cut. If you need extra sympathy, try pouring salt or lemon juice into the wound.

    o **Black Eye**: Hold this book in your hand. Close your eyes. Think peaceful thoughts. Then whack yourself in the face with the book. Keep repeating until your eye is swollen and discolored. (Helpful hint: If you can't see out of your eye, chances are that it's swollen and probably discolored.) When someone asks you what happened, follow this formula:

    - **Men** say, "You should see the other guy."
    - **Women** say, "Don't nobody touch my man!"

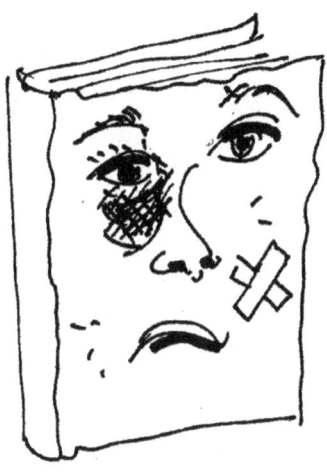

o **Damaged Testicle**: This one is just for the guys. First, pull down your pants; let those low-riders hang free. Next, open this book and place it just below your testicles. You'll want to take a deep breath. Think happy thoughts. Now slam the book shut. Repeat until you pass out. This is not an injury that most people will see, so you'll have to explain the damage when people notice you walking with a limp. You might be thinking that you can just walk with a limp and tell others that you have a damaged testicle without actually doing the deed, but you're not that good an actor.

- **Beat aggressive grapes to a pulp.** A single grape on its own might not act tough, but put them in bunches and they can be quite intimidating... especially the ones from Tuscany. The next time those seedless ovals get under your skin, place them between the pages of this book and slam it shut. That should knock the Manischewitz out of them. You might wind up with an everlasting chardonnay stain on your precious book, but let that serve as a warning to future offenders looking to put you in a jam.

- **Take your mind off of the nice weather, the beautiful people and the ocean while at the beach.** Everywhere you look there are exhibitionists showing off their amazing bodies. The waves keep coming and coming and coming ashore. And that imperious sun won't let up! Don't you just want to get your mind away from it all? Good thing you brought along this absorbing book; it will numb your mind faster than a Ke$ha single. You won't be distracted anymore by that topless woman with the amazing rack, or that guy peeing on his friend with the jellyfish sting, or the music and laughter from that amazing luau taking place just 12 feet away from you. It's just you and your literature… the way the beach was always meant to be enjoyed.

- **Practice your bartering skills.** Before the invention of currency, goods and services were traded only for each other. Then paper money was invented, Bernie Madoff was born, and everything went to hell. So let's get back to the good old days. Leave your wallet at home and see how much you can get for this book. Will you fetch four apples or six oranges? How about a haircut or an oil change? Don't sell yourself short… everyone loves a good book! That *Slumdog Millionaire* DVD might be out of reach, but a couple of David Hasselhoff CD's should be in play. I'm sure most people will be happy to accept this book in lieu of cash; after all, both are made of paper. And money can be so pretentious. Who reads Latin, anyway?

- **Practice your balancing skills.** It's never too late to become a supermodel, but every supermodel needs to have certain abilities. For instance, they need the ability to survive on only five crackers a day. They need the ability to control their bowels while talking to Anna Wintour. But most of all they need the ability to balance a book. Start with the basic task of balancing this book on your hand; first with your right hand and then switch to your left. Pretend you're carrying a tray of little cocktail weenies. Next, try balancing this book on your foot. This will take a little more practice. Feel free to watch Brazilian soccer players for inspiration. Next, can you balance the book on your butt? I didn't think so. But keep trying. You may want to eat a lot of fatty foods, in order to increase the size of your butt (don't worry; this is not considered cheating). Finally, you are ready to try balancing this book on your head. Place it on your head and walk slowly in a straight line. Just place one foot in front of the other. Once you get the hang of it you may want to pick up the pace and even attempt walking in circles. Next, try chewing gum while you walk with the book on your head. Hop on one foot. Skip. Do the Electric Slide. Congratulations... you are now a supermodel! Quick fact: Supermodels are allowed to date writers of books. Just in case you were wondering.....

- **Exercise.** We all want to look and feel healthier (except Michael Moore), but we still like to eat a lot of food. To counter this behavior, we must exercise. Joining a gym may be expensive, but using this book is free... once you or somebody else has already paid for the book. Here are just a few ways it can assist you to get in better shape:

    o **Curls:** Hold the book in your hand and curl your arm into your body. Return your hand, with the book, to its original position. Repeat. In fact, repeat frequently. Try to do 100 in each hand, counting one at a time, like this... 1, 2, 3, 4, 5, etc. If you can't do 100, try counting five at a time, like this... 1, 5, 10, 15, 20, etc. This will make it much easier to do 100. If you still can't do 100, try counting 20 at a time, like this... 1, 20, 40, etc. Doing it this way could mean it takes a tad longer for you to see the desired results.

    o **Ankle Weights:** Going for a walk in your neighborhood is a good workout, but going for a walk in your neighborhood with books strapped to your ankles is even better. Strapping a book to your ankle makes your ankle heavier... which makes it harder to lift... which makes you burn more calories. It's physics; try not to think about it too much. Authors particularly love this form of exercise, because you'll have to buy a second book for your other ankle. Make sure that the books are strapped with the covers facing out, so that everyone will be able to see and appreciate your taste in literature.

o **Wrist Squeezes:** No matter if you're holding onto a lasso or a ledge, you'll need a firm grip. Take this book in your hand and squeeze. Release and then squeeze again. And repeat. Try squeezing with each hand for about five minutes. If that feels too easy for you, try squeezing the book with your feet. When you master that, you have my permission to start biting the book. Really work those chompers. In fact, if you bite hard enough you will get fresh book juice, which is known to be rich in minerals and cure cancer.

o **Measure Your Gut:** It's important to keep tabs on how much weight you're losing / gaining / ignoring. While this book can't act as a scale, it can help you measure your stomach fat. With one hand, grab your gut and squeeze. Don't cheat; really get a good handful. Now, with your other hand hold this book under your gut with the cover flat against your hip. Note the page number that your gut extends to. Keep checking during the following weeks. Soon you'll be bragging to your friends that you've dropped from a page 85 to a page 40!

• **Fend off an angry dog.** Now you've done it. You just had to taunt the neighborhood dog with ground beef and a dead kitten carcass, didn't you? Now he's on the loose and out for blood. You'll never outrun such a magnificent beast, and I doubt you'll be able to properly convey the concept of irony to him. Face it, you're about to be attacked. Unless you have a craving for rabies, you'll need to act quickly. Hold this book out in front of you. When the angry dog attempts to bite you, shove the book in his mouth. If that doesn't stop him, take the book and whack the dog until he runs away. (Please note: I am <u>not</u> suggesting that you take the book and hit random dogs with it, unless it's a Chihuahua.) You can also use this book in the same manner to fend off a horny dog. No means no, Fido!

- **Protect yourself in a prison swordfight.** For this exercise, you will need some additional items. First of all, you will need duct tape or glue in order to attach the book to your body. You will also need a sword, because without one you may find yourself at a major disadvantage in a swordfight. Finally, you will need to go to prison and make some enemies. Place the book over a vital area of your body, such as your chest or genitals. Don't worry about your shins; anyone who goes after your shins in a prison swordfight is just being a dick. For a proper demonstration, check out the 23-minute mark of the classic American feature film, *Ricochet*, starring Denzel Washington and John Lithgow. You'll notice that books are the popular choice for body armor, while newspapers seem to offer rather little protection.

- **Wrestle an alligator.** You won't win. Just because you can do something, doesn't make it a good idea. Sure, you can wade into the grimy Florida Everglades and challenge the first alligator you see with only this book as protection. You can try lulling the reptile into a sense of serenity by reading a few chapters before you strike. You can jam this book down the alligator's throat as you're grabbing it around the neck. But understand that it won't work. You'll lose the fight and it will eat you. And in the process you will lose a perfectly good book.

- **Show people that you don't know karate.** In this age of Facebook and Twitter and your blabbering sister, people must think that they know everything about you. But is that really true? While it's a given that everyone has heard of your yodeling skills and most have probably seen that tattoo of Sonic the Hedgehog riding a gremlin, I'll bet the overwhelming majority of the population probably doesn't know about your complete incompetence when it comes to martial arts. To set the record straight, get a large group of people to gather around you; try standing on a table and shouting for them to come closer while you wave your arms in the air. Then pick one person to hold this book. He or she should hold the book with one hand on each side, so that it provides a nice, flat target for you. Now, attempt to break the book in half using only your bare hands. Don't hold back... give it your very best karate chop. When you fail to break the book in half, everyone around will know that you, in fact, do not know karate. If they're still not convinced, you may also attempt to break the book in half using your foot, elbow or head.

- **Show people that you do know how to read.**
Before everyone walks away thinking that you're a total loser, make sure they stick around long enough to hear you read the rest of this paragraph. Repeat these words: *I (state your name) may not be very good at karate, but I do know how to read.* For proof, keep reading this book out loud to them until each and every one is convinced. Not only will they be impressed with your sixth grade reading skills, but they will appreciate the entertaining work of art that you have just chosen to share with them. But don't read past this chapter. Make them buy their own book!

What <u>can't</u> I do with this book?

With all of the amazing uses for your new book that have been presented, you might find yourself asking: *Is there anything this spectacular book can't do?* First of all, how dare you! Second, I'm afraid there are a few rather insignificant tasks this book will fail to achieve for you. Hey, nobody (or book) is perfect. Hopefully you won't feel the need to attempt any of these activities. Hopefully you'll have some alternatives. Hopefully you will spend the rest of your life in a comfortable, secluded room with only this book. But if you do want to try any of these tasks, you're on your own:

• **Poach an egg.** I'm just going to put this out there: anything that involves a stovetop or any other source of fire probably won't be a good match for this book... or any other book for that matter. Also not a good match for this book: eggs. Remember, someone bought you a book of jokes... not yokes. So any activity that combines eggs with a flame is not going to fly with us. Feel free to read this chapter while you are waiting the three minutes or so for your egg to "poach"; just don't ask this book to help you do any of the cooking or wash dishes afterwards.

- **Play the violin.** Your big recital is going to start in just a few minutes, but you've forgotten your bow at home. Perhaps you shouldn't have stayed up so late playing the Leonard Bernstein drinking game last night. Unfortunately for you, this book does not play the violin. It is way too thick with important knowledge for such a slender instrument. Instead, perhaps you should try playing a larger apparatus. I hear the bass is available, or how about the tuba? That guy in Def Leppard plays the drums with only one hand; surely you can play them with a book instead of drum sticks.

- **Program your universal remote.** It's bad enough that you're eschewing a book for your television / DVD player / radio / video game / remote-control drone / iPad / blow-up doll. Now you want help in setting up all of that other crap? I don't think so! Good luck trying to read those directions in Korean... unless you're actually in Korea; then they're probably written in North Korean... which means they're covered in blood and step one is actually a plea for food. Or you can go back to Radio Shack and once again give your zip code to the uninterested 19-year old who is just trying to make it to the end of his minimum wage shift so that he can smoke dope and watch re-runs of *Baywatch*. Maybe you can ask your neighbor for help; the same neighbor on whom you called the cops last weekend for throwing a raucous kegger that lasted until 3:00 in the morning. Or perhaps your aunt, who will quickly turn this conversation into an inquisition as to why you're still not married at your advanced age. None of these people were there for you when you were stuck in an elevator for two hours last year, or when you needed something to keep your mind occupied while waiting for your phlebotomy appointment last month. That would be your trusty book, which you are now tossing aside in order to play *God of War III*.

- **Conduct electricity.** This book is filled with information and knowledge, but it is not filled with metal. No copper, no silver, and certainly no gold. (*I know what you're thinking. The other day you were reading this book and decided to eat a peach... one of those peaches your mother had bought earlier in the day... the ones that you were warned would need a few days to ripen. But you couldn't wait, so you bit into that tempting peach; only it was so hard that your gold tooth fell out of your mouth and into the pages of this book. I'm sorry to tell you this, but that tooth fell out of the book this morning while you were practicing your trampoline act for the annual Hillel talent show. By the way, your act is looking fantastic!*) So this book can't act as an extension cord or antenna. On the bright side, this book is a much safer option to have in the bathtub with you than a television, a toaster or Lorena Bobbitt.

- **Gut a fish.** I know that you're excited about catching that catfish off the Mississippi coast. It only cost you a boat rental, a case of beer, nine hours of your time and a sunburn on 80% of your skin. But before you can enjoy a tasty fish fry tonight, you'll need to find another way to gut and clean your dinner. This book may perform miracles, but it doesn't perform surgery. Even if the pointed edges were sharp enough to cut through the skin of the fish, do you really want to get blood all over the pages? This is a messy job; use something that you won't mind damaging forever, such as a Sears catalog or a Jackie Collins novel. This book can still be of use catching other fish. Just lure them to the surface of the water by reading a few pages, and then club them over the head with the book to finish the job.

- **Insulate you from electricity.** Just because this book is not a conductor of electricity, does not mean that it will shield you from a giant volt. Your desire to keep reading this book during a massive lightning storm is understood and appreciated, but you should not do so under a tall tree. Perhaps inside a car would be safer (and drier) for you. And even with this book in one hand, you should not stick a metal fork into a wall socket with the other. And under no circumstances should you hold this book and lick a light bulb; trust me... they taste horrible.

- **Get the Cubs to the World Series (again).** Don't even think about it. Forget we brought this up. It's a complete waste of time. Nothing... and I mean NOTHING can get the Cubs to the World Series! (again) Ernie Banks couldn't do it, Ryne Sandberg couldn't do it, and Lou Pinella couldn't do it. If the Cubs were playing only themselves in a close game, the St. Louis Cardinals would <u>still</u> win. In 1969, they blew a 9.5 game lead in less than a month to a New York Mets team that had never even finished above .500 before. The Cubs finally added lights to Wrigley Field in 1988, but their fans still preferred to watch them in the dark. This franchise was cursed by a goat... a freaking goat! We drink their milk! We let our 3-year old daughters pet them at the zoo! There is nothing this book can do for your pathetic franchise (again). Even if it could throw a 97 mile an hour fastball with its left hand (just pretend the book has hands), it would probably sign with the Yankees. On the bright side, at least this book will be able to entertain fans in the bleachers during yet another embarrassing 15-3 blowout loss. Enjoy 2016... for the next 100 years.

- **Understand Albanian.** More than six million people in the world speak this language, so perhaps you should ask one of them to help you instead. Albanian is full of extra, unnecessary letters and syllables that tend to only complicate matters. I can't understand a word of it, and quite frankly I'm not sure I even want to. Just look at some of their most famous people. John Belushi starred in a movie (*Animal House*) about a bunch of guys who only go to college for the parties. What sense does that make? Everyone knows that college is first and foremost for higher education. His brother, Jim, starred in the "hit" television show, *According to Jim*, for eight seasons. Seriously.... EIGHT SEASONS!!! Who can possibly make sense of that? And then there's Mother Theresa. She spent her entire life helping other people. Who does that?! I don't understand any of it.

- **Cure herpes.** What happens in Vegas, stays in Vegas. Unfortunately, you didn't have enough money for Vegas... and what happens in a Mexican strip club men's room does not necessarily stay in a Mexican strip club men's room. Now you've managed to score a hot date back home and your crotch looks like a pepperoni pizza that was left out in the sun for a couple of weeks. I'm sorry to tell you that this book can't do much to get rid of the warts, nor can it offer much protection for an intimate moment. On the bright side, you can hide your shame by holding the book over your crotch while you undress with the lights off. And if that doesn't work and your date leaves you to wallow in shame, at least you'll have something fun to read while you wait for Cinemax' late night programming to begin.

- **Deflect bullets.** Apparently, you've picked a fight with the wrong gangster. Maybe you thought this one would have a good sense of humor about his mother's homemade lasagna recipe, but it looks like he's going to take your insult to heart. Now you find yourself going for a ride deep into the woods, with nothing but this book and loose bowels to keep you company. In a few minutes you'll be begging for your life with a gun to your head. One thought would be to put this manuscript over your head for protection, but that would be a mistake. Think of this book like Switzerland; it doesn't like to get involved in other people's disputes… especially when one of those people is a gangster who has a gun. Besides, we all know that you're going to die anyway. Better to die with your dignity and book intact.

- **Give her an orgasm.** The good news is that this book can stay hard (cover) for hours. The bad news is everything else. Physically, this book shouldn't get too close to her... um... womanhood, as paper cuts downtown tend to be a bit of a mood killer. Emotionally, the only thing we promise to stimulate is her mind. Below the neck you're on your own. And don't even ask about the G-spot. Everyone knows that's just a myth. Why don't you just ask us to find Waldo or a straight musical theatre actor? They don't exist! Instead of an orgasm, give her some flowers or a nice piece of jewelry. She'll survive. I'll bet she wanted a unicorn when she was a kid and didn't get that either. Don't feel guilty. Women are used to living with disappointment.

- **Break your fall.** As you leap off that bridge and plummet towards the Earth at a reckless speed with nothing but a thin cord wrapped around your left ankle for safety, hoping the cord will hold and wondering if it should fail, will your favorite book be able to break your fall... know this: Yes. It would be able to break your fall and save your life... but it will choose not to. Next time you feel the urge to get your adrenaline pumping, you can simply turn to the next chapter. Start now...

What type of book is this?

There are just so many choices when it comes to books nowadays, and unfortunately your husband / wife / friend / daughter / son / cousin / uncle / aunt / brother / sister / co-worker / therapist / butler / stalker / prized pupil / landlord / blind date / henchman doesn't really know you all that well. Good thing for you this can be whatever type of book you want it to be. Here are just a few examples:

Romance:

Edith looked deep into the eyes of her soul mate, Francisco. She longed to tell him the truth, to lift the burden of guilt that she had been carrying in her breast all of these years. She wanted to break down and cry in Francisco's arms, begging her lover for forgiveness and swearing upon her grandmother's fortune that she would always be true to him and him alone. Edith opened her mouth, that dreadful secret so close to finally escaping through her soft, supple lips. Seconds felt like hours; time standing still as beads of sweat soaked her porcelain skin. Francisco stepped closer and leaned into Edith, his breath clinging onto the side of her neck as he whispered in her ear. "Don't you worry," Francisco reassured in his thick Guatemalan accent. "I know about you and

Jean-Paul. I've always known. I used to stand by the river and throw rocks at the passing salmon to ease my pain. But ever since he died in battle I knew you were mine. I forgive you. I need you. I love you." And with that Edith was freed from worry, flying off the ground into the arms of her merciful lover. Francisco kissed her passionately on those soft, supple lips as the two of them collapsed into the grass. He moved his hand slowly up her leg, caressing her thigh and tantalizingly close to her most sacred place. For the first time in almost a week, Edith felt like a woman. Today there would be no more talk of Jean-Paul... no more talk of regret... of vampires or werewolves. Today was for love... for a passion that words could not possibly explain... and then a long nap.

Murder Mystery:

The building went dark. A blood-curdling scream could be heard throughout the halls of the library. And when the lights were turned on again the body of poor Miss Wilson lay motionless in the center of the room! Jackie, the shy high school sophomore, checked for a pulse. "She's dead," Jackie announced. Frightened sobs filled the room. Who would kill such a lovely old librarian? The rain outside intensified. It was clear that nobody would be able to leave the library any time soon, which meant the killer was still amongst them! Could it be Sister Mary, the sweet nun who tutors homeless children? Or perhaps Tyrone, the local drug dealer who uses the free internet to email rivals that he intends to *pop a cap in that ass*? It's anybody's guess. Skip Helms carefully surveyed the scene. Skip hadn't worked the beat in more than a decade, since his partner was gunned down in front of a Winchell's doughnut shop, walking away and never looking back. Truth be told, he didn't miss it a bit. But now things were different. Skip stared into the vacant eyes of poor Miss Wilson. She was giving him the same look as his late partner, only without the crumbs of a Boston Crème hanging on her bottom lip. He kneeled down next to Miss Wilson and closed her eyelids. "Don't you worry," Skip promised. "I'm going to catch the scumbag who did this to you." And with that he sprang into action.

Children's Book:

Ronnie the Rattlesnake wanted a cookie. After all, Ronnie had been a very good rattlesnake lately. He had gone an entire week without making noise, which is very hard for a rattlesnake to do. Ronnie slithered into Timmy's house. He could smell the freshly baked cookies sitting on the counter in Timmy's kitchen. "Hey Timmy," Ronnie begged, "Can you toss me a cookie?" Timmy looked down at Ronnie and shrugged his shoulders. "Sorry, Ronnie. Mom won't let us have any cookies until after dinner." Ronnie slithered over to glance at the clock on the microwave. It was only 3:00; that means dinner is a whole three hours away! Ronnie started to cry salty rattlesnake tears.

"Please, Timmy... I won't bother you again. Just accidentally knock a cookie on the floor and I'll do the rest." "No way," Timmy exclaimed, "She knows how many cookies there are. I'll get caught and she'll beat me! Last time I was in a coma for two weeks!" "Please," Ronnie moaned, "I don't ask for much, Timmy. You're my best friend in the whole wide world." "You killed my brother!" Timmy screamed. Ronnie felt bad as Timmy sobbed over the cookies. He gently wrapped himself around Timmy's leg. "Hey Timmy," Ronnie soothed, "I'm sorry. I didn't know that the venom would kill him. I was just playing around. I thought your Mom would care enough to suck the poison out of your brother. But I didn't realize that he was adopted and that your mother wouldn't want to smear her lipstick. She really is a mean lady. Please stop crying. You're getting the cookies soggy." Timmy threw the entire plate of cookies on the ground and ran out of the room in tears. Ronnie the Rattlesnake finally had his cookie, and nobody even had to die this time.

History:

The Chinese Boxer rebellion rose out of a fierce anti-western sentiment during the late 19th century. Due in part to the weakness of the Qing dynasty and fears that western influence would destroy traditional Chinese culture, the Boxers murdered hundreds of western diplomats and Chinese Christians. This peasant uprising began with a secret society known as the Yihequan, or "Righteous and Harmonious Fists." They would eventually be called Boxers by the westerners, based on their boxing rituals which the group believed would make them invulnerable to

bullets. The uprising began in the fall of 1899 in the countryside, eventually spreading all the way to the capital of Peking (now Beijing) by the spring of 1900. Some 140,000 strong, the Boxers would hold Peking hostage for almost two months, before an international army could recapture the city. The international army consisted of more than 2,000 soldiers from the United States, Great Britain, France, Italy and other nations. Once Peking was secured, the western powers were able to impose their will on the already weakened China. Eventually, this would pave the way for the Republican Revolution of 1911, which overthrew the emperor and turned China into a republic.

<u>Yearbook:</u>

OMG! Senior year has been SOOO much fun! You are such a slut! LOL! I promise we will always be BFF's... pinky swear! We look SOOO fat in our photos! LMAO! Good luck in the merchant marines! I am SOOO sorry that I slept with your boyfriend! KIT!

Joke Book:

Ladies and Gentlemen, I now present to you… <u>The Greatest Scottish Joke Ever</u> (authentic Scottish accent not included):

A young American tourist is enjoying his first visit to Scotland. He takes in the sights of Edinburgh, looks around Glasgow and takes some photos in Loch Ness… but he still finds himself missing something. In search of understanding true Scottish culture, the young man gets on a bus a travels for hours into the countryside. Eventually he finds himself in a small village, seemingly untouched by the luxuries of modern civilization. He walks another couple of miles down the road and comes across the local pub. It doesn't take long for the bartender to spot this outsider. "You're not from around here," says the bartender. "No sir," confesses the tourist. "I'm American, just looking for some real Scottish culture." "Well," exclaims the bartender. "Just buy old man McGregor there a pint and you'll get all the Scottish culture you could ask for." So the tourist takes a seat next to old man McGregor and orders a couple of pints. For the next 20 minutes the old man ignores his free pint, simply staring off into space. The young tourist is just about to give up his pursuit, when the old man finally speaks up. "You see that fence out there," McGregor cries while pointing out the window, "I built that fence with me own bare hands. I cut down hundreds of trees, nailed them all together, sanded them, painted them, varnished them… that fence will last a lifetime, but do they call me McGregor the fence builder? Nay." And with that the old man finally acknowledges his pint and takes a sip. Another 10 minutes pass. The old man speaks up again. "You see that pier out there," he again points out the window, "I built that pier with me own bare hands. I traveled two months into the forest, pushed a mighty boulder back to town and into the lake, covered it with wood, weather-coated the wood… that pier will last for centuries, but do they call me McGregor the pier builder? Nay." And with that the old man gulps down the rest of his pint. Not even 30 seconds pass before McGregor pipes up again, almost shouting this time. "You see this bar right here," the old man pounds his fist on the bar, "I built this bar with me own bare hands. I traveled six and a half years into the forest, chopped down the mighty oak, dragged it to this very spot, cut it down the middle, sanded it, varnished it… you can see your reflection in it. This bar will last for generations. But do they call me McGregor the bar maker? Nay!" The old man sighs.

"But you fuck one goat…."

Travel:

While only a small percentage of us may qualify for Harvard University in Cambridge, the splendid town of Harvard, Illinois welcomes everyone. With a population around 10,000, Harvard is located on the upper reaches of the Kishwaukee River Basin, only seven miles south of the Wisconsin border. Lodging options include the Morning Glory Bed & Breakfast on Route 14 and the Heritage Inn & Suites on South Division Street. Harvard also boasts a plethora of fine dining options; its many accredited restaurants include McDonald's, Taco Bell, Subway, Little Caesar's and Dairy Queen. Kelly's Restaurant and the Bigfoot Inn, both located on US Highway 14, provide the palate with a more local fare. The town's aquatic center entices visitors with basketball hoops, a zero depth pool with slides, a sand play area and snack bar. While any time of year is ideal for a visit to Harvard, you won't want to miss out on Milk Days, the state's longest running annual festival which takes place on the first weekend of June. It started as a small tribute to the dairy farmer in 1942, but has grown to attract more than 100,000 people each year. Fun events include the pancake breakfast, the antique tractor and talent show. But the highlight of the festival has to be the Milk Drinking Contest, which is clean lactose fun for the entire family. There are three different age groups, with the heavyweights (18 & older) drinking an entire quart of milk! Cookies are not included.

Reference Book:

NATION	CAPITAL
United States	Washington, D.C.
France	Paris
Ireland	Dublin
China	Beijing
Peru	Lima
Oz	Emerald City
Grenada	St. George's
Luxembourg	Luxembourg City
Malaysia	Kuala Lumpur
Finland	Helsinki
Cambodia	Phnom Penh
Middle-Earth	Gondor
Lebanon	Beirut
Canada	Ottawa
Jamaica	Kingston
Iceland	Reykjavik
Krypton	Kryptonopolis
Egypt	Cairo
Germany	Berlin
Brazil	Brasília
Kenya	Nairobi
Pandora	Tree of Souls

Sports:

If Satan ever decides to build a hockey rink in hell, you can bet that it will have a New York Islanders logo at center ice. Over the past seven years the Islanders have finished last in their division six times. In 1999, they finished the season with the worst record in the entire league, which included an expansion team from Nashville. Nashville! This was appropriate, since Islanders fans are often more depressing than country music played backwards. This franchise was once sold to John Spano, a swell guy who just didn't happen to have any money in his bank account; unlike previous team owners who were only morally bankrupt, this guy was actually bankrupt! The Islanders let Mike Millbury run the organization for 10 years, during which time he failed to draft any impact players, gave $140 million to an unmotivated Alexi Yashin and briefly changed their logo to look like the Gordon's Fisherman. Today, Millbury does commentary for NBC's hockey coverage... because apparently the Grim Reaper wanted too much money. When the Islanders finally scraped up enough garlic and a silver cross to axe Millbury, his replacement was none other than back-up goaltender Garth Snow. I don't mean that Snow was a back-up goaltender a few years earlier; I mean THAT MORNING. And his very first move as general manger was to give their starting goaltender, the solid but oft-injured Rick DiPietro, a

15 year contract extension. Surprising to nobody at all, DiPietro spent the following seasons battling more injuries before finally being released. In 2013, they traded a first-round draft pick and popular winger Matt Moulson for Thomas Vanek, who would score the exact same number of goals as Moulson before spurning the Islanders in free agency for Minnesota... a place where hamburgers and hot dogs come with a side of frostbite. In 2014, their franchise center, John Tavares, sustained a serious knee injury while playing for Team Canada in the Olympics. Maybe the Islanders did win four Stanley Cups in a row during the 1980's, but this kind of feels like saying General Custer won a bunch of battles against the Native Americans during the 1860's.

Biography:

Angela Lansbury was born in London, England in 1925. After moving to Hollywood during World War II, Ms. Lansbury would establish herself as one of the greatest actors of the 20th century. She was nominated for an Oscar in 1944 for her very first film, *Gaslight*. Although Ms. Lansbury was nominated for a dozen straight Emmy awards without a single win, she has accepted plenty of other hardware during her illustrious career. Ms. Lansbury has garnished five Tony awards, six Golden Globes and a People's Choice award. She was recognized with Lifetime Achievement awards from both the Screen Actors Guild and the Television Critics Association, and was the Hasty Pudding Theatricals' Woman of the Year in 1968. Ms. Lansbury has not one, but two stars on Hollywood's legendary Walk of Fame. On Broadway, she originated the role of Mrs. Lovett in *Sweeney Todd* in 1979 and the title role in *Mame* in 1969. In Hollywood, popular works include *Dorian Grey*, *Bedknobs & Broomsticks*, *The Manchurian Candidate* and the cult comedy, *Something for Everyone*. Despite her tremendous success in both theatre and film, Angela Lansbury is best remembered for her long run on the hit television show, *Murder, She Wrote*, from 1984 to 1996. She remains an entertainment icon, serving as a mentor and inspiration to younger actors across the globe. Angela Lansbury became a United States citizen in 1951.

__UNAUTHORIZED__ Biography:

Angela Lansbury is a mean old witch. She gives out dried fruit to kids on Halloween, and has never tipped more than a dollar to the guy delivering her pizza. Often Ms. Lansbury would call telethons and make large pledges to the cheers of all the volunteers, only to hang up before they could ask for her credit card number; she would then go back to betting on cock fights and burning books. Her performances on Broadway were breathtaking, but backstage Ms. Lansbury could be very difficult. She was particularly tough on her assistants, once demanding an Almond Joy without the almonds. When her assistant suggested that she just try a Mounds instead, Ms. Lansbury scoffed, "Mounds are for hacks like Chita Rivera!" Perhaps Angela Lansbury is best known for her starring role on the television series *Murder, She Wrote*. On screen she may have come across as a sweet lady, but in reality the cheap miser was always complaining about paying actors to play dead bodies. "Why do we have to pay these talentless stiffs scale?" she would whine. "We can just kill a homeless person for free." The series would eventually be cancelled when a behind the scenes murder involving a caterer could, in fact, not be solved. Today Angela Lansbury lives in an old shoe by the sea, firing her riffle at any adorable sea otters who dare come too close to her property. I heard most of this from a friend of a friend's stoned nephew... so I'm pretty sure it's true.

Cookbook:

Today we will be making **_Cajun Pasta with Meat Sauce_**.

Ingredients:

- Pasta
- Meat Sauce
- Cajun Seasoning
- Water
- Salt
- Olive Oil
- Large Pot
- Strainer
- Wooden Spoon
- Stove

Take the large pot and fill it with water, then place it on top of the stove. Add a pinch of salt to the water and place the cover on the pot. Then turn on the stove and bring the water to a boil. Try not to stare at the pot, as a watched pot never boils. (Reading a good book will help you pass the time.) When the water boils, remove the cover and add a dash of olive oil. Make sure that you remove the cover <u>before</u> adding the olive oil to the pot. Now put your pasta in the pot; if the pasta does not fit into your pot, you can break it in half.... the pasta, not the pot. Stir the pasta gently with the wooden spoon for about 10 minutes. Turn the stove off and empty the contents of the pot into the strainer over the sink. Remember that the water will still be very hot, so now is probably not a good time for the old "strain pasta over the sleeping roommate" prank. Once the pasta is strained you are ready to place it in your bowl / plate / casserole dish / bundt pan / coffee mug / batting helmet... or other object you will be eating out of. Pour the meat sauce (personally, I prefer Ragu's fine selection) over the pasta and sprinkle some Cajun seasoning on top. Enjoy!

Self-Help:

It's been a tough year. You lost your job. Your husband / wife / platonic tease / escort / boyfriend / girlfriend / pen-pal / ho left you. Your dog died. Your favorite show (*Blossom*) was cancelled... again. And Justin Bieber won't stay off the radio. Sometimes you think it would be better if you just ended it. Listen to me: <u>Don't do it</u>! Inside that punching bag exterior is a beautiful person. Don't believe me? Go on over to that mirror and take a look at yourself. Go on. Don't be shy. Nobody's looking. Just stare at that gorgeous face! How about a smile? Just a little one... tickle, tickle, tickle... there we go! Aw, you're beautiful. Let your hair town / take off your wig / put a wig on. Do it. Now take your clothes off. Do it. Slowly. Yeah... take it all off. Oh, baby. Now dance. Slowly. Aw, yeah. Look at that. Go outside and show off those goods. Do it. I said DO IT! Show everybody that beautiful body. Boy, are you talented. Run up and down the block, screaming "Look at me! I'm naked and beautiful!" at the top of your lungs. I'll bet you're starting to make some new friends. Feeling better? You betcha! In fact, you've never felt so alive. Now go buy this book for all of your depressed friends. Right now. Do it. Don't look back. Run to the nearest book store. Nobody wants to know where you are hiding your wallet right now.

Pop-Up Book:

You're walking through the forest. The grass is green. The trees are tall. You turn the page and.... WHAM!!! Look at that tree!!! It's jumping off the page at you! You get around the giant tree and can see a village in the distance. You turn the page and... WHAM!!! A castle!!! It's so big! You are now in the kingdom of Cadbury. They are getting ready for a big party. You turn the page and.... It's just another page. They are setting a giant banquet table with turkey, duck, pheasant, pig and grape juice. A show is about to begin. You turn the page and... WHAM!!! It's a giant lute! You could reach out and play it if you like! The entire village is dancing to the music. The royal family has stopped by to join the party. You turn the page and... WHAM!!! It's the king's severed head! Someone has killed the king! It's madness at this party! You see the princess standing alone. She's very distraught. Her father is dead. You go over to console her. You tell her that joke about the flying dragon and the sickle. She gives you a smile; I think she's feeling better. The princess invites you up to her room. She takes off her dress. You turn the page and... WHAM!!!

2002 Saab 9-3 Owner's Manual:

The turbo gauge indicates the air volume for combustion, which is equivalent to the engine load. At low loads, the needle will move within the white zone. At higher loads and during heavy acceleration, the needle will enter the yellow area. At very high loads (certain variants only) the needle may enter the first part of the red zone without indicating that there is a fault. Under certain barometric conditions the needle may enter the first part of the red zone without necessarily indicating that a fault has arisen. If the needle repeatedly enters the red zone and the engine at the same time loses power, because the monitoring system is holding the charging pressure down, you should contact an authorized Saab dealer. If the speed exceeds 143 mph (230 km/h), the increase in speed will be limited by the lowering of the boost pressure. The pressure gauge then moves towards the middle of the orange zone, indicating reduced engine output and thus reduces the speed of the car as well.

Magazine:

April is thrilled to follow in the footprints of her mother and great-aunt to grace our pages. April is a speech communication major who describes herself as "outgoing, fun and perky." Her perfect evening includes "Lots of soft music with a man who is ready to please me." She likes girly pleasures like shoes – seriously, who doesn't – but also enjoys whistling and taxidermy. Dislikes include "warm beer and guys who bite while kissing." Vital stats: 34-24-35.

What? You said you enjoy these for the articles, right?

Memoir:

I remember the day Ronnie the Rattlesnake killed my brother, like it was yesterday. We were all waiting for the cookies my mother had just baked to cool off. Ronnie was a rather friendly rattlesnake, but sometimes he could be a tad domineering. He suggested we play a game of tag, and bit my brother, Abdul, as his way of declaring Abdul "it." I can still hear Abdul's shrieks of pain, like it was yesterday. Abdul fell to the floor, Ronnie curled up in the corner and I went running for Mother. It had always saddened me that Abdul and Mother never got along. Mother was in her powder room applying makeup for the annual "Save the Marshmallows" fundraiser. I told her that there had been an accident and that Abdul urgently needed a doctor. I can still picture that annoyed look on her face, like it was yesterday. Mother had just applied her nail polish, so I dialed the phone for her and held the receiver up to her ear. I could distinctly remember hearing the doctor advising her to suck out the poison, but for some reason Mother pretended not to speak a word of English. After I hung up the phone, Mother checked her lipstick, patted me on the head, and promised to attend to Abdul after the party. I can remember seeing that her fingers were crossed in the mirror's reflection, like it was yesterday. I went back to the kitchen and tried to suck the poison out myself, only my infant sucking glands were too weak. Three days later Abdul passed away... surrounded by me, Ronnie, a couple of guys from immigration services, and a plate of oatmeal-raisin cookies. While I struggled to get over my brother's passing, Mother seemed to do a very good job of hiding her grief. It only took her a matter of hours to convert Abdul's corner of the basement, where he used to sleep, into a sewing table that she would never use. Mother would always try to cheer me up with a declaration of "Abdul, who?" each time I woke up screaming in the middle of the night from one of my guilt-laden bad dreams. I would eventually learn to suppress my pain, until a few years later when Mother was checking her makeup while crossing the street and was run over by the tour bus for KISS. I can still remember that sickening squishing sound of the wheels running over her, while *Detroit Rock City* blared in the background, like it was yesterday. After that, it was just me and Ronnie. That's when we left home to join the circus.

<u>Satire</u>:

I am not familiar with this format.

What did I do to deserve this book?

I can understand if guilt has started to set in. By now you must be realizing the true enormity of the treasure you hold in your hands. Are you truly worthy of such knowledge... such fun... such love? Yes, yes and yes. You most certainly are! While nobody in this world may be perfect (that goes double for those of you in Sarasota), you have earned the privilege of reading these words... and these words... and those words... which are still these words. A good deed here, a mitzvah there, and it all adds up to a hero with whom I am happy to share this book. Still doubting yourself? Let's take a trip down memory lane:

• **Remember that time you opened the door for that pregnant lady?** (It shouldn't be hard; you only did this once.) You were in a rush to get your teeth bonded, but that lady was really, really pregnant and walking towards the door. She looked like she could barely stand... let alone walk... let alone open a door all on her own. You held the door open for what seemed like an eternity as she gradually waddled past you. It was a very nice action on your part! So what if you're the one who got her pregnant? So what if you never spoke to her again? So what if you moved across the country under an alias in order to avoid paying the court-ordered child support? You still opened that door. When you open a door, you open your heart... and are therefore allowed to open these pages.

- **Remember that time your backseat nagging helped avoid a car accident?** Sure, for several years your constant shrieks of "Watch the road!" and "Use your turn signal!" and "Don't hit that carrier pigeon!" accomplished nothing but to annoy your daughter and son-in-law. But how are they finally going to give you a grandchild if they're splattered all over the street? Then on that fateful Arbor Day a few years ago, you found yourself to be the only one paying attention to the road from the backseat, as the kids argued over whether or not it was time to put you in a home. You were the only one who noticed that a giant moving van was not slowing down to stop at the approaching four-way intersection. You screamed out to your son-in-law, who swerved just in time to avoid certain disaster. You saved their lives! You were parent of the year!

Too bad they still decided to put you in a home. If you had a hard candy for every day that your family hasn't come to visit you... wait, you <u>do</u> have a hard candy for every day that our family hasn't visited you, and then some. At least you also now have something enjoyable to read on your breaks from Sudoku.

- **Remember that time you performed CPR on your neighbor's cat?** Whiskers was a cute little fellow, but he had an annoying habit of climbing on your roof and falling asleep inside your satellite dish. (If the poor cat wanted to use your satellite dish to get some sleep, he could have just watched *Big Brother*.) Then came that fateful Saturday afternoon. You were watching college football, when you heard a shriek and a loud thud outside your window. Before the invention of TiVo you would have simply ignored every loud shriek heard outside your window, but now you could actually pause the game and investigate the noise. Outside you found that poor, lifeless ball of fur lying in between the daffodils and the azaleas. Without hesitation you breathed nine new lives into your neighbor's pet. Unfortunately for you, Whiskers was faking it. Your would spend the next three months trying to get the taste of tuna and liver out of your mouth, all because that perverted cat just wanted to get some attention. Free yourself of your shameful past with a light-hearted book, and let's never discuss this disturbing incident again.

- **Remember that time you tipped the delivery guy a dollar?** It was Christmas Eve. It had been snowing for three consecutive days. There were tornado warnings in effect for the area, that nearby volcano was about to erupt, and aliens were preparing for their invasion of planet Earth. A good number of people would have been concerned with more than their appetite, but you had the munchies after smoking dope for the entire afternoon. Good thing your internet held out just long enough for you to place your order. The pizza delivery guy made it about halfway through the four-hour drive to your house in his Nissan Versa before it broke down, and then traveled the rest of the way on foot. Some people would have complained that their pie was frozen when it finally arrived. Some people would have wondered why this high school freshman with horrible acne deserved a tip at all, but you had a heart. You noticed his effort and his frostbite, and you generously gave this brave delivery guy a dollar. That's 100 cents! Then you sent the young man back into hell. We may never know why he didn't make it back to the pizza shop that night / following morning / apocalypse, but we do know that wherever he was able to finally seek shelter… he did it with an extra dollar in his pocket. That evening you feasted on pizza; tonight you can feast on this book, with an extra topping of knowledge.

- **Remember that time you switched from whole milk to 2%?** It took you months to adjust to the new watered-down taste of your cereal, and your gourmet coffee became almost impossible to swallow. Your sacrifice was the wise decision of a responsible adult; one that will eventually help to extend your now miserable life. Even though you still include bacon in every meal and enjoy snacking on frozen sticks of butter, your switch to 2% milk officially wipes the slate clean. Those little percentages of fat you save will add up over the years, which eventually equates to a person who is 100% deserving of this book. Just don't place it anywhere near your coffee. That stuff is crap now.

- **Remember that time you called 911 while an elderly man was getting mugged?** Old man Donnelly had just cashed his social security check, and was now on his way to spend it on horses and booze at the track. It would have been a wonderful Tuesday afternoon for old man Donnelly, until he was confronted by two girl scouts who pushed him up against a brick wall and forced him to turn over the money. You witnessed the entire incident from behind a parked car. You called 911 and reported the crime, and even took photos on your cell phone. The one thing you did not do was attempt to stop the muggers yourself, because those girl scouts can kick really hard and you love their cookies. By the time the police arrived, old man Donnelly was left with a bunch of bruises, some spare change and a handful of thin mints. No matter what old man Donnelly says, it's not your fault that the assailants got away. You're still a hero in my book, although I can certainly understand if you do feel a slight amount of guilt. After all, old man Donnelly is your father.

- **Remember that time you cured AIDS?** You were only trying to cure athlete's foot. One day you dissected the wrong lab rat and ZING... you became Magic Johnson's best friend. Not only has your vaccine saved millions of lives, but it has also made you filthy rich. Among your many prized possessions now are a yacht, a Ferrari, a mansion in Monte Carlo and a very special person who had the good sense to purchase this book for you. Now you have something to read on all of those long flights to Africa, where you've become even more popular than Bono! Gee, it must feel good to be you... except for that itching sensation inside of your shoe. You really do need to get back to finding a cure for athlete's foot.

- **Remember that time you let a total loser get to second base with you?** Matthew in IT couldn't spot a boob if you drew him a map to the nipple. He had crooked teeth and a bit of a perspiring problem. Your love life might have been stuck in neutral for a while, but at least you still had some standards. Then came the bi-annual office holiday party. You started the evening with your eyes on a couple of cute boys in sales, but three hours and six whiskey sours later you and Matthew were getting it on by the copy machine. Perhaps you were distracted by the horseradish breath or the romantic sounds of Matthew clearing his sinuses, as he slid his sweaty hand up your blouse. This moment of passion quickly came to an end when Matthew's mother called to inform him that he was breaking curfew. It was a night to forget, except for that terrible hangover and all of the photocopies that were plastered around the office the next day. This book can't wash away your shame, but it can keep you company on all of those job interviews you're sure to be going on in the near future.

- **Remember that time you did <u>not</u> feed the animals at the zoo?** You were eating a delicious pasta primavera near the giraffe exhibit. One of the giraffes kept looking down on you with those sad giraffe eyes. You looked deep into those sad giraffe eyes, which of course were windows into a sad giraffe soul… a sad giraffe soul that had never tasted your mother's sensational pasta primavera. Perhaps a person without your convictions would have allowed that giraffe to taste a new delicacy that day, but the sign posted next to the giraffe's electric fence clearly stated that you should not feed the animals. And so you finished your meal and even licked the plate clean, all while managing to block out the steady stream of giraffe tears that were falling from above. You even described in great detail the euphoric sensation of each bite, just so your helpless audience could truly appreciate the glory of your incredible meal. It was a nice gesture when you bought a handful of bird seed and offered that to the now suicidal giraffe as a consolation prize. Nobody could have guessed what it would do to your hand in return, but hey… you still have another one to hold this book, and those scars on your face are starting to heal nicely, too.

- **Remember that time you left a note at the scene of the accident you had just caused?** You were driving 80 miles per hour in the snow… backwards… from the passenger seat. It's hard to believe that you would clip a parked Escalade, but that's exactly what happened. Nobody was around to witness the accident, but you showed true maturity by leaving a note on the parked car's windshield. It would have been nice if the note you left behind included an apology or your name and contact information, instead of simply stating the following: one pint of orange chicken, two pepperoni pizzas, three tacos and an order of flapjacks. Hey, a note's a note. Maybe one day the owner of the car will hire a hand-writing expert and find you. But until that day comes, you can rest assured that you did your part. Take a load off and enjoy this book, preferably from the backseat of a cab.

- **Remember that time you had perfect attendance?** You were in the eighth grade. You showed up for every class. You showed up with fevers and chicken pox; in rain and snow. When there was a fire drill you remained firmly in your seat. When most of your friends skipped class to watch Kim Kardashian make a sex tape next door, you told them you would wait for the next one. When your teacher joined your friends in watching Kim Kardashian make that sex tape next door, you offered to teach the (now empty) class. You even showed up during spring break, just in case there was a mistake on the school calendar. Sure, you were teased by the other students, the faculty, the principal and your own parents... but at least you didn't waste any tax dollars. For that you received a paper certificate at the end of the year, a thousand wedgies, and now a wonderful book. Speaking of books, perhaps it's time to stop using your school locker. After all, it has been 20 years.

- **Remember that time you deleted those naked photos of your ex-girlfriend?** It was the best birthday present you could ask for (aside from this book); your sweet little lady wearing nothing but silk stockings and a sombrero. It was a wonderful night of passion, and you have the photographic evidence to prove it. Three months later she's dating a wealthy ventriloquist, and you're stuck with nothing but memories... and those lascivious photos. A lesser man / lesbian / Larry Flynt would have posted those pictures online and shared them with all of us, but you.... wait a minute.... what the hell were you thinking?! Don't you get it? You'll never get those pictures back! They're gone now! Every day you'll forget a little more about what she looked like naked... and some of us will <u>never</u> get to see her naked! She's dating a wealthy ventriloquist now! The rest of us are out of her league! Screw it... You don't deserve this book, but since you've already got it keep reading and we'll forget this conversation ever happened... Idiot.

- **Remember that time you released the fish you had just caught back into the water?** After five long hours of drinking beers under a hot sun and fishing for trout, you finally caught one! You reeled it in, clubbed it a few times with a bowling pin, painted it to look like the flag of Ireland and posed for a slew of pictures with it. But then you had a choice: gut the fish, get blood all over your favorite Adidas sneakers and cook it... or toss the trout back into the water. Since you can't gut a fish with this book — as discussed in a previous chapter — and don't eat fish, this wasn't a difficult decision. You mercifully allowed the trout to live... that is, after you had re-painted it to look like the flag of Australia and posed for a few more pictures.

You gave that beautiful creature the gift of life, which it then relinquished by repeatedly impaling itself on a bed of coral. Apparently, the emotional scars of its terrifying ordeal on your boat were too much for the trout to bear. But at least you had a fun time.

- **Remember that time you didn't steal money out of your mother's purse?** It was just sitting there on the counter, enticing you to do a little one-stop shopping. Your mother was taking a nap upstairs, resting before it was time to start her second of three jobs that she works on a regular basis to support you. Soon you would have to wake her up, so that she could prepare you a proper dinner before heading out to the coal mines. Just another 20 minutes of avoiding temptation is all it takes to be a good son / daughter / neighbor's kid / goldfish / ALF, and........................... so close.................. be strong..................... fight the urge.......................... and..........................you did it! Way to go! You didn't take the money! You should be very proud of yourself. Pat yourself on the back. Wait... So you <u>did</u> take the money? All of it? Every penny, huh? Well, at least you're planning to use that money to buy her something nice, right? Perhaps something classy, like a book? Oh, you're going to spend it on crystal meth. I guess that works, too. After all, she just wants you to be happy.

- **Remember that time you were the designated driver during Mardi-Gras?** The bars were packed with horny young adults slurping down margaritas and hurricanes, but you were stuck drinking nothing but diet cokes. You were finally hitting it off with a cute girl from Apalachicola, when your buddy interrupted to inform you he was ready to leave. By the time you turned your attention back to the girl, she was already making out with the bartender. Thus at 4:00 in the morning, you found yourself driving 10 miles per hour down Bourbon Street, dodging puddles of vomit and masturbating clowns. Women tried to distract you by pressing their bare breasts against the windshield, while your buddy hooked up with a witch-doctor in the back seat. For your trouble you received a New Orleans Saints keychain, a bunch of pretty beads (which should do you a lot of good back home in Schenectady) and this book. At least you didn't get crabs.

- **Remember that time you shared your fabulous green bean casserole with the neighbors?** Five cans of green beans, two cups of almonds, a stick of butter and a pinch of deliciousness makes your green bean casserole famous throughout the land. You were planning to save your leftovers for another meal, until your neighbors knocked on the door. They were friendly and smelled like famine, and 20 minutes later your famous dish was nothing more than a tasty memory. Your neighbors were so grateful, they promised to stop letting their dog urinate on your front lawn. You fed their hunger; now this book will feed your soul. Besides, it will give you something to read while waiting for those neighbors to return your hedge clippers, power tools, lawn ornaments, antenna, goldfish, wedding dress, kitchen sink, ceiling fan, grandmother.......

- **Remember that time you sat through all THREE HOURS of *Pearl Harbor*?** I honestly have no idea how you did it. I mean, it's not like you were handcuffed to your seat. The exit doors weren't bolted shut. You had the freedom to leave the movie theater, but instead you reached deep down into your soul and found the intestinal fortitude to sit there and watch the entire movie... even the credits! What I'm saying is... you could have left. Other people left. Lots of people left. Some people threw up in their seats, then left. Some people left and then jumped in front of a bus, then rolled the remains of their crippled carcasses off a bridge, and then shot themselves on the way down. You... for whatever insane reason... stayed and sat through three excruciating hours of mind-numbing dialogue, like this:

> *Rafe:* *You are so beautiful it hurts.*
> *Evelyn:* *It's your nose that hurts.*
> *Rafe:* *I think it's my heart.*

And this:

> *Danny:* *Which way ya goin?*
> *Rafe:* *Uh, right, no left. Left. I'll go left.*
> *Danny:* *Okay, we're goin left, right?*
> *Rafe:* *Right, right?*
> *Danny:* *Right, like we're goin left, or right like we're goin right?*

> Rafe: Well, now you got me all mixed up, I dunno make up your mind!
> Danny: God, Rafe, we're goin right. Righty-Tighty!

And, dear lord, this:

> Lt. Col. Doolittle: Where'd you find religion?
> Doolittle Co-Pilot: When you assigned me to this mission, sir.
> Lt. Col. Doolittle: I want you to do me a favor.
> Doolittle Co-Pilot: What's that, Colonel?
> Lt. Col. Doolittle: Pray for both of us.

Only Michael Bay could take an esteemed actor such as Alec Baldwin and make him play a character named "Doolittle." He took a movie about one of our country's most harrowing moments and turned it into a soap-operatic love triangle; it was like watching the bastard love child of *Top Gun* and *Bridget Jones' Diary*. This movie was so terrible, the folks who made *Team America* devoted an entire song to it. The plot had more holes than four rounds of golf. Yet, you kept watching. Even during the third hour... when they flew to Japan after the attack, got shot down, captured by the enemy and then escaped during a seven-second gunfight... you watched all of it. Not only do you deserve this book, I'm pretty sure you deserve a medal. At least you got to see Josh Hartnett die. (Okay, it was just the character he was playing; but it was still nice.)

- **Remember that time you whistled for a cab for that elderly lady?** It was cold enough to make dentures chatter. Hailing a cab was going to be extremely difficult for the old woman, who needed to keep both hands on her walker as it slid across the icy sidewalk. Good thing you had your trusty whistle on hand. One ferocious blow and there was a taxi at your feet with the meter running. You opened the door, looked at the old lady with a loving smile, and then got in the cab and drove off. You shouldn't feel guilty, as there was probably a bus stopping by any minute. Who are we kidding? You're going to hell.

- **Remember that time you gave blood... then bone marrow... then a kidney... then a lung?** First you got roped into giving blood during a blood drive at your office. When you were finished, they gave you juice and cookies. You love juice and cookies! Soon you were giving blood every week. Then you read an article about some poor little girl who needed bone marrow. If you got juice and cookies for some measly blood, just imagine what you could get for bone marrow. So you gave your bone marrow, saved that girl's life, and most importantly... got a free dinner, with desert and everything! The following year, you found out that your cousin needed a kidney. You never really cared for your cousin, but he was really desperate and willing to give up a share of his upcoming inheritance... once he took his mother off of that pesky respirator. You took the following year off, in order to spend your new fortune traveling around the globe. But during a visit to the Far East, you learned that an underground Cambodian crime lord was willing to pay top dollar for a new lung. You figured that since you were born with two lungs and this rich guy only needed one... why not? Besides, it would be just like giving the blood, bone marrow and kidney. Other organs will probably be able to help you breathe... like your gallbladder or pancreas. It's a good thing that you have this book now. I'm pretty sure physical activity is no longer an option for you.

How can this book help me pick up women (or men)?

You are fortunate to be reading the Barry White of books. This manuscript has paired many souls over the years. Antony and Cleopatra... check. Napoleon and Josephine... you bet. Fred and Wilma Flintstone... absolutely. The pages you are currently holding in your hands are responsible for all of these romances, which is simply amazing when you consider they hadn't even been written yet. Just imagine what this book can do for you! If you've been lucky in love, you're about to get luckier. If you don't know the difference between a red rose and a black widow, don't worry; this chapter will guide you all the way from initiating conversation, to making your move, to changing your identity the next morning. Think of this as your very own personal Craigslist page, only without the transvestite midget spanking posts. Whether you're looking for Adam or Eve, just take a seat in the garden and soak in this knowledge (and leave the apple alone).

*** This book recognizes that not every man is looking for a woman and not every woman is looking for a man, and appreciates customers of all orientations. That being said, your tome finds heterosexuals to be in much more urgent need of dating advice... especially the ones still using OK Cupid. ***

Let's start with the ladies. Hello, gorgeous. I understand that you're trying to get a man's attention. Good for you! You're making the world a better place. The first thing you will want to do is figure out which part of you is the most appealing to men. If you think it's your mind or your sense of humor, you are wrong. It's definitely a body part. Now, if you have trouble figuring out which body part is your best feature, just ask some guys. Don't worry; they will be happy to judge you. Here's a hint: It will most likely be your breasts, eyes, butt, breasts, hair or breasts. If you find out that your best assets are your feet, this book advises you to get breast implants. Now that you know what to flaunt, here's how you can use this book to tempt the object of your affection:

o **Eyes:** With your Prince Charming sitting in front of you, hold this book over your face and giggle. Then lower the book just low enough to frame those beautiful peepers for a moment or two, before covering your face again. Repeat as necessary.

o **Hair:** Sitting next to your obsession, follow these steps:

- <u>Step One</u>: Start out by reading this book with your hair covering your face.

- <u>Step Two</u>: Seductively brush your long, flowing locks away from your face and give him a smile.

Now, if you do not have a pretty face, this book advises that you still follow step one… but skip over step number two. Also, if your hair is not long enough for step number one, you should probably wait about a year before attempting the above method of seduction.

o **Breasts:** Put on a low-cut top. If you don't own a low-cut top, you can either go out and buy one or make one using a pair of scissors. Next, make sure your future husband is standing in front of you. This is very important! If he is not in front of you, the following move will not be as effective. Facing him, drop this book on the ground. Feel free to add an "oops" for extra effect. Then bend over to retrieve the book. Under no circumstances should you bend at the knees.

o **Butt:** For this maneuver you will want to be wearing a tight pair of pants or a really short skirt; it simply depends on how desperate you are. You will be performing the same exercise as for breasts, only you will want your Doctor McDreamy to be behind you for this one. While you don't need to wear a low-cut top for this exercise, the book feels that it can't hurt your chances. Again, do not bend at the knees. If it takes you less than 10 seconds to retrieve this book off the ground, you're doing it wrong.

If none of the above moves gets the attention of your man, you might need to be a little more assertive. Take this book and drop it on his foot. Write your phone number / email / twitter handle / inmate number / dental records on the inside of the book and then hit him with it. He'll eventually get the message.

Gentlemen, now it's your turn. What is your best feature? It's probably not a body part, but based on your IQ / Inkblot / SAT / eHarmony score there's not much else to work with. Part of this will depend on what kind of shape you are in. Stand up straight, holding the book in your hand. Now drop the book to the ground. Look down. Do you see the book?

No: You are <u>not</u> in good shape. This will rule out your best feature being your stomach, butt or chin.

Yes: You might be in good shape. But can you bend down and pick the book up without pulling a muscle?

> **No:** Not so fast! This will rule out your best feature being your legs, back or testicles.
>
> **Yes:** Stop showing off.

Let's just pretend you're in decent shape. If your gal hasn't run away screaming at the pathetic sight of you yet, you must have *something* going for you, right? Here are a few areas we might try to exploit for your benefit:

o **Arms:** Women like a strong man. Whether that bulge by your bicep is lean muscle, soggy fast food flab or a rolled-up sock, use what's there to call the attention of your mail-order bride. Hold this book with one hand and flex. Make sure the lady is somewhere in the same room as you. Now grunt. Relax your arm and repeat. Start counting as your turn the pages.

o **Butt:** You will want to follow the advice for the ladies above, but without the short skirt. Try not to grunt while bending over or scream when you throw your back out. Above all else, and no matter how difficult this may be for you, do not pass gas!

o **Mustache:** First, you will need to grow one. Don't worry, we'll wait………………………………………………
………………………………………………………………
……………………………………………………….. good.
Sit next to a pretty lady with this book covering your face. Find something amusing in the book (shouldn't be hard) and sophisticatedly chuckle as you lower the book. Stroke your mustache. Twirl it in your fingers. Take a sip of scotch. Inhale flavored smoke from a wooden pipe. Find a breadcrumb tucked away in the hairs and toss it to a hungry pigeon. If this lady is not mesmerized by your handsome 'stache, you might need to move to Brooklyn.

Face it, the easiest way to impress a woman is to convince them that you are the one who wrote this book. Go ahead, pretend that you're me; I won't mind. If she doesn't fall for it, chances are that she's probably too smart for you anyway. Don't worry if this route doesn't lead you to paradise; there are still plenty of other options. Now, there's some good news and bad news. The good news is that about 10% of us will be able to pick up ladies with our sensational good looks; the bad news is that the rest of you will need to work a little harder if you want to take a lady to the Promised Land. Those 90% of you who fell out of the ugly tree will need to dust off your romantic bones and charm the ladies into your scrawny little arms. Master the language of love and your gal will be swooning in no time. Here's a fact: women absolutely LOVE poetry. Normally they only fall for dead poets, but you're going to be the exception. Don't know any poems? Not to worry; Cyrano will help you out. Here are a wide variety of poems that are sure to break the ice:

Roses are red, violets are blue
With this book, it is you that I woo.

Roses are red, violets are blue.
An evening with me, is one you won't rue.

Roses are red, violets are blue.
You'll find I fit nicely, like an old worn-in shoe.

Roses are red, violets are blue.
You're sweet like honey, I'm Winnie the Pooh.

Roses are red, violets are blue.
I'm not your first choice, but your options are few.

Roses are red, violets are blue.
(Long, awkward stare/silence)

Roses are red, violets are blue.
We go together, like bagels and Jews.

Roses are red, violets are blue.
My prostate might be aging, but my Ferrari is new.

Roses are red, violets are blue.
I'm going to the hoop, like Bob McAdoo.

Roses are red, violets are blue.
Violets are blue. Violets are blue. Violets are blue.

Roses are red, violets are blue.
Ooo, ooo, aah, aah… it's mating season at the zoo.

Roses are red, violets are blue.
I'm the ghost of Pleasureville, here to say "Boo."

Roses are red, violets are blue.
I tested negative, how about you?

Roses are red, violets are blue.
I long for your love, but I'll take pity too.

Any of these are sure to sweep your girl off her feet. For any women who would like to try the poetry angle in order to woo their guy, here's one that's sure to work:

Hello.

If that poem is too long for you to memorize, feel free to try this one:

Hi.

If that one is still too long for you, just blink at him. I'm pretty sure this is how Brigitte Nielsen nabbed Flavor Flav. After all, Flav isn't really known for his extensive vocabulary, is he?

So now you have a date. Mazel Tov! Guys, this is where things get even trickier. You are about to experience the longest dinner of your lives. You did a fine job picking out that fabulous French / Chinese / German / Mexican / Cuban / Vietnamese / Kosher restaurant, but now you will only have a few short hours / minutes / seconds to make a great impression on her. You should make sure that you pack your wallet, breath mints, this book and more breath mints… just trust me on this… and please stop holding this so close to your face when reading.

Here are just a few ways your favorite book will help you get from dinner to desert:

Are you vertically challenged? Do you still get into movies for half price? Do you need a step-ladder in order to set your oven? Are you tired of asking for a booster seat at the restaurant? Now you don't have to! Sitting on this book will make you appear taller and allow you to look your date in her sultry eyes. Even better, the more books you buy, the taller you'll be!

While silently staring at your date throughout dinner might arouse a handful of women (especially in Germany), the majority of them will expect you to initiate stimulating conversation. Here are a few topics that are sure get the chit-chat going:

> o **Find out if she has any dead relatives.** Bringing this subject up might be a little tricky, but once she starts talking about her grandparents / mother / father / aunt / uncle / evil twin, you won't have to say another word for the rest of the meal. Just nod your head and look sympathetic, and hand her your napkin when she starts to cry. Pour her another glass of chardonnay. Perform a séance at the table. Pretend you harbor the spirit of her dead relative, and that spirit insists she go home with you.

o **Talk about the weather.** This one might be a little boring, but it's something you will both have in common. Everyone experiences the weather. If you're not affected by the weather, you're probably dead. Discuss how this perfectly wonderful day was affected by rain / snow / hail / wind / volcanic ash / locusts / reindeers falling from the sky. You'll be surprised to learn how much the two of you have in common… even if it's that you both hate talking about the weather.

o **Show her how much you love sports.** Women love passionate men, and nobody has more passion than sports fans (especially the ones from Green Bay). You should paint your face in your favorite team's colors. If that doesn't impress her, tackle a busboy. While waiting for your appetizers to arrive, see if you can get her to do the wave. Just don't talk about the WNBA. After all, people are eating here.

o **See if she has a rather large "ex".** This could possibly be the woman of your dreams, but let's not get pulverized here; after all, you're no good to anybody with a broken face. Ask if she knows any big fellas who can help you move a piano. See if she follows the lumberjack games. Find out if she's dated a Biff, Axel or Jean Claude. Just to be safe, you should probably walk home with one eye open and become an organ donor.

o **Discuss today's therapy session.** This will be a good way to find out what's on her mind. She might be a little reluctant at first, so tread gently. You may find that having her stare at a shiny object while you dangle it from side to side will help. If she still won't divulge anything about her session, you could always talk about yours. For starters, tell her how much she reminds you of your mother.

Ladies, you can also use this book to gain favor with your date. For instance, let's say he takes you to an outdoor fish market and there are flies fluttering all around. Now, imagine that one of those flies actually lands on your man's face. Most women would simply point to the fly or gently try to shoo it away, but you are not most women; you're better. Now kill that fly for him. Take this book, close your eyes and swing the book as hard as you can. (Please remember to clean the fly's guts off of the book after you have succeeded.) And if you miss the fly, you can always read aloud from this book to your date while you are patiently waiting for him to come out of his coma.

Once you have committed to each and every piece of advice in this chapter, don't be surprised when your date suggests that you move the evening's festivities to his or her house / apartment / car / tent / cardboard box. Leave a nice tip for the waiter at the restaurant, but do not leave your book! There is still more advice to be had at your fingertips. For instance, a lot of men have great difficulty in making their move. They will sit next to a beautiful woman for hours, nervously sipping their Amaretto Sour and babbling about *Galaxy Quest* until their frustrated date loses hope and kicks them out. Here is a guaranteed way to avoid an unfulfilling end to your date:

During the date, try to act a little clumsy. Now, don't spill a drink on her or anything rash. Trip over a crack on the sidewalk or drop your fork once or twice. Basically, you just want to lay the foundation that you are a little uncoordinated. Then, when you're back at her place, sit next to your lady on the couch and offer to read to her from your book. (Obviously, she will accept this request.) As you are starting to read, you just "accidentally" drop the book over her shoulder. Lunging for the book, you will wind up on top of her... and passion will ensue.

While having sex with your partner... thanks to this advice... you can still use your book to shield you from distractions. (You can also use it to shield you from other things, but that would be messy.) Throw it at a light switch or an alarm clock or a nosey roommate. Your roommate can then read this book to take his / her mind off of you having sex. You can also use it as a pillow, a paddle, a nightstand for your glasses or earrings, a nipple clamp and a diaphragm.

Finally, guys... if your date does not end on a positive note and you are worried that you might have blown your chance, your book can help make sure that you see each other again. Just leave the book at her place, and then you will have an excuse to go back. But don't wait too long to contact her. Once she starts reading this, she's likely to keep it for herself!

What other gifts would I have received, if not for this book?

You are one of the millions (or soon to be millions) of lucky recipients of this life-changing manuscript. If only each and every one of your neighbors were as fortunate. They received other, less impressive gifts. It might be frightening to think about what other gift your mother / father / son / daughter / cousin / aunt / uncle / warden / Drivers Ed instructor / neighbor's book publisher / mathletes arch-rival / girlfriend / boyfriend / cartoon dog / husband / wife / lover / ex-lover / ex-husband # 1 / ex-wife # 4 / co-worker who stole your top-grossing account would have purchased for you in place of this awesome book… but let's take a look at some of their weaker options. Try not to be scared, but you may want to hold on tight to your book as you read these:

• Since the generous person who bought this book for you was probably in a bookstore, I'm guessing that they might have bought you **another book**. It could have been any type of book. It could have been about Shakespeare or Snooki. It could have been about winning championships or the Los Angeles Clippers. It could have been written by Jackie Mason or it could have been funny. Talk about a crapshoot!

- Of course, bookstores don't just sell books anymore. There are plenty of other worthless items for sale. Most of them will fill a stocking, but none of them will fill your soul:

    o **Bookmark:** While it may serve a purpose, this placeholder contains slightly less words than the actual book. It's also smaller and, thus, easier to lose. Besides, you don't really need a bookmark… just an abnormal knack for remembering page numbers.

    o **Chocolate:** One gift will bring you sweet, pleasurable satisfaction; the other is chocolate. This book will go right to your brain, not to your thighs. And while some unfortunate people are allergic to chocolate, nobody is allergic to reading… unless Mel Gibson is holding a Torah.

o **Calendar:** Don't be fooled by all of the pages; they're almost exactly the same. Like my mother used to say, once you've seen one month you've seen them all. This is also a good time to point out that while a calendar has a lifespan of only a single year, this book will last a lifetime. Unfortunately for you, that is also a single year; you should really wear more sunscreen.

o **CD:** Just because you can party like it's 1999, doesn't mean you should. Not only is the CD outdated; it's also dangerous. I'm just saying, Spice Girls never wrote a book. Neither did Ashley Simpson. If you really want something pleasant to listen to, just read this book out loud.

- Perhaps your special somebody would have tried to find something else with the same measurements as this book, since it's one size fits all.

  o **First-Aid Kit:** Talk about your pessimistic gifts! The person who gives you this must be secretly hoping for you to experience a horrible accident. The only time this gift will come in handy is when the recipient is so upset about receiving it that they slash their own wrists. Just for the record, paper is very good at absorbing blood... and this book has a bunch of pages.

  o **DVD:** I'm sure that *American Gigolo* is enjoyable to watch the first seven or eight times, but after that it will become completely useless. You would also need a DVD player and a monitor, while this book can be enjoyed without an electrical outlet. Try watching *Gigli* while at the beach or in your prison cell.

  o **Underwear:** The person who gives you this better have an engagement ring or a positive urine sample. Panties might be sexy, but they can only be enjoyed sporadically. You can read this book every day for a year, but you can only wear that thong four or five days in a row, tops.

o **Magnet:** This horrible gift can only be enjoyed in one room of the house. You are much better off with a more portable book. Besides, if you really wanted something that suctions itself to the refrigerator night and day, someone could have just gift-wrapped your father-in-law.

o **One Adult Sneaker or Two Baby Sneakers:** You would look pretty stupid wearing only one sneaker around town, unless your name is Henry Hoppitytot; in that case, people will understand. The baby sneakers won't do you a lot of good, unless you are a baby. In that case, you should really be focusing on your education… I'll bet a book would help you with that.

o **Alarm Clock:** Every night you dream of that perfect little villa on the edge of the Mediterranean, only to be woken up by that mean-spirited little box blaring Don Imus at you first thing in the morning. This book will let you sleep for as long as you like, leaving you free to tend to those fake olive trees and work on your imaginary tan. And when you get fired for not showing up to work, you'll have plenty of extra time to read!

o **Program from *Starlight Express*:** There's nothing you can find in that program that you can't find here. The director thanks the actors. The actors thank their parents. Everybody thanks Andrew Lloyd Webber, but nobody thanks the person who taught them to roller skate. Oh, and everybody's going to Sardi's after the show.

o **Pack of Napkins:** This is like receiving a small book; only without all of the big words... pretend it was written by Paris Hilton. Hey, you can wipe your face with any number of other items. Try using your sleeve, your socks, your friend's sleeve or your framed picture of Margaret Thatcher.

o **Sandwich:** Who put mayonnaise on this? You hate mayonnaise! It would have been a delicious concoction of ham, cheese and pickles... but somebody had to screw the whole thing up with the wrong condiment. This book may not come with chips and a fountain soda, but it can also be enjoyed dry (like your sense of humor).

o **Tape Measure:** There are certain things in life that cannot be measured, and the joy you experience with a wonderful book is one of them. Besides, you've been told over and over again that size isn't that important.

o **Notebook:** Here is a book that you have to write yourself. Some gift! Next, they'll be inviting you to dinner at a supermarket. They probably didn't even give you a pen or pencil. So prick your finger and try to write something clever in blood; quickly, before you pass ou........

o **Gift Certificate:** If they really cared about you, they would have given you cash. Your wallet is already full with a dozen credit cards, pictures of your kids / cats / altar boys, and that Taco Bell club card. If you try to stuff one more card into your wallet, you might not be able to close it! We all know that you would have just used that gift card to buy this book anyway, so the least they could do is cut out the middle man.

o **iPad:** The problem with getting an iPad is that.... well.... you see... Who are we kidding? An iPad would have been pretty cool.

- Your homeboy / homegirl / houseplant might have just forgotten to get you anything, then ran out to the local liquor store at 5:00 in the morning... looking to trade in that old Betamax remote for an acceptable gift... or even an unacceptable gift. Does it really matter at this point? I mean, its 5:00 in the morning... and they're trading in a Betamax remote! At this point you should probably just be happy with whatever you get:

    o **Booze:** It might sound tempting to hang out with your pals, Johnny Walker and Jose Cuervo, hunting for Wild Turkey in Malibu. But when Miller Time is finally over and your head is pounding harder than Charlie Sheen at Hedonism, you'll wish that you had just stayed in for the night with a good book.

    o **Lotto Tickets:** Just what you need... another reminder that you're not a millionaire. And if you are a millionaire, what on earth do you need with more money? There are very few gifts in life that are priceless, and this limited-edition book is one of them. Besides, you don't need anything else to scratch after what you already did to that scab on your inner thigh.

o **Cigarettes:** Like your book, these are made of paper, are highly addictive and will leave you short of breath. Unlike your book, they will eventually kill you. Allow me to explain. One day you will be smoking your precious cigarettes outside of a raucous karaoke bar. A man with a ponytail will notice you smoking and ask if you have another one to spare. Of course you will refuse to share, because you can't go around handing out smokes to every guy with a ponytail who pesters you for one. Unfortunately, it will turn out that the guy with the ponytail is in fact the son of a vicious Colombian drug lord. You'll run for your life and escape in the hull of an old cargo ship bound for Vietnam. After sustaining yourself for a week on plankton and drinking urine (don't worry; it's not yours), you will settle into a comfortable life in Hanoi trading silk goods for bacon. Eventually, you will learn that the Colombian drug lord has decided he can make more money in investment banking and his son went blind after challenging an ostrich to a dance-off. You will safely return home, reunite with your old flame, adopt a few kids and live a life of pleasure in the suburbs... where 30 years later you will die of lung cancer.

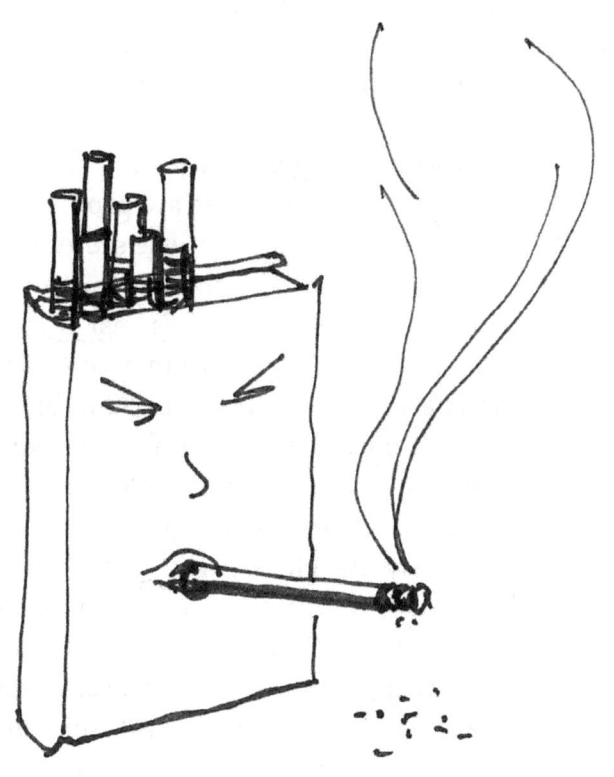

- There is a very slight chance that your gift buying decision maker might have chosen to purchase this incredible book over something a tad more expensive. Take a look at a few of the curses you were fortunate to avoid:

    o **Diamond Earrings:** First of all, the only men who should be wearing these are professional athletes... the good ones that use steroids and charge money for autographs. As for the ladies, diamonds are not always a girl's best friend. Pretend you're wearing your fancy schmancy new diamond earrings to your local Wendy's; after all, you can't purchase a junior frosty wearing just anything. You sashay into Wendy's wearing your sparkly accessories and order your meal. Unfortunately, the elderly woman working the register is hard of hearing, so you have to lean in really close for her to hear you properly. You're only a few inches away from her face, when you slip on a stray chicken nugget. As you stumble towards the elderly cashier, it's hard to pinpoint the exact moment when your diamond earring slashes her jugular. The spraying blood not only takes the poor woman's life, but also your appetite. Now you're left to deal with a sore left ear, a potential lawsuit, and a three week ban from your favorite fast food restaurant.

o **New Car:** There are many advantages to owning a car, such as the ability to get from one place to another. For instance, traveling from New York to Boston takes five hours in a car; on foot it takes about 27 years. However, your excitement over a potential new Hyundai Elantra might be blinding you to all of the hazards that come with owning a new car. You'll still have to pay for insurance, oil changes, gas, parking tickets, speeding tickets, bumper stickers and other expenses. You'll also have to drive the car, which means no more sleeping on the highway. And now you'll also have to put up with all of your annoying friends begging you for rides to and from the roller disco. Face it... you would have probably totaled that car within a year. So you have a book instead; a wonderful book that will happily keep you company on the bus.

o **Sex:** Hooray, sex! SEX! S-E-X!!! And with a partner this time! For one night you get a little action, and your hamster gets a well-deserved rest. There isn't much downside to this gift... at least for the next nine months.

Chances are that you received this book from a real cheapskate. It probably didn't come with a card. It probably wasn't even wrapped. And it probably had already been read by the person who gave it to you, although who can blame them for that? Speaking of re-gifting, one final chapter of knowledge lies ahead...

How can I re-gift this book?

So not only are you too cheap to purchase a new present for your mother / father / son / daughter / bartender / grandma / grandpa / aunt / uncle / accompanist / cousin / step-brother / favorite stripper / boss / professor who's about to flunk you / sister / grandchild / that was f-l-u-n-k you / secretary / best friend / ex-wife / TSA agent who was very gentle with you behind the partition, but you're also willing to part with your wonderful book? How dare you, sir / ma'am / RuPaul?! Fine... You've got to do what you've got to do. Your options for re-gifting your new toy are limitless, but since this book has to end eventually here are just a few:

• The concept of re-gifting this book... or anything for that matter... is quite simple. Go to the store and buy some wrapping paper; if you can't afford wrapping paper, you can use a newspaper. If you do choose to wrap the book in a newspaper, it's suggested that you use the comic section. You can also use the sports section if they're into sports or the horoscope section if they like to blame all of their problems in life on astronomy. Wrap the book nicely (you may even add a bow or ribbon), and hand the book to the lucky individual and tell them that this gift is from you. There... it's that easy. Your ruse will be much more successful if this book is in good condition. Research shows that most book stores will not sell books with missing pages, torn covers or sections marked in pink highlighter. Although book stores are starting to get rather desperate, so I wouldn't put anything past them at this point.

• You will notice that the cover of this book has a blank line (ie: _____) where the recipient's name should be written. If the line on your book is still blank, it means that the person who gave you this treasure did not care enough about you to spend five seconds writing in your name. Lucky for you, this has made the task of re-gifting much simpler. Take a pen, or a fine point magic marker, and write the name of the fortunate individual for whom you are planning to bestow this book on the line. It will help if you know the person's name, as you only get one shot at this procedure. Remember that once you take this important step, the book will no longer be yours. You may want to pour yourself a strong drink to help cope with your impending significant loss.

• If the person who originally gave you this book had the audacity to care about you and write your name on the blank line mentioned in the section above, it will make your re-gifting task a lot harder. Don't panic... all is not lost. Your trusty and soon to be discarded book is here to guide you through the necessary steps to complete your shameful task. There are still plenty of ways that you can pass this bundle of knowledge onto another worthy individual. It may take some creativity on your part, but since you've already shown the capacity to get out of buying a new gift for someone... I have confidence that you are up to the challenge.

> o The first recommended step is to find another person who shares the same name as you. Being an average Joe, Tom, Jen or Sam has never been so wonderful. You Hann-Jings, Latishas and Dicks might want to have a conversation with your parents over this particular disadvantage. If you like to go by your last name instead of your first name, you can still pawn this book off on another member of your family... or perhaps a

different family that happens to have the same last name. Hey, you might even wind up meeting a long lost relative!

o You can change the name on the cover of your book by adding an extra letter or two. It may not look pretty, but you never had good penmanship to begin with. You can tell the recipient that you were nervous when writing their name on the line, because they mean so much to you. The ability to stammer and shed a couple of fake tears will add a nice touch to your performance.

- *Jo* can become *John* or *Josh*.
- *Evan* can become *Evangeline*.
- *Michael* can become *LeMichael*.
- *Joseph* can become *Josephine*.
- *Don* can become *Donna*.
- *Brian* can become *Briana*.
- *Marc* can become *Marcellus*.
- *Brad* can become *Brady*.
- *Van* can become *Vance*.
- *Shane* can become *Shanequa*.
- *Son* can become *Sonny*.

o If you can't add extra letters, try changing the letters that are already there. You'll be surprised how adding a line or an extra curve will transform a useless letter into one that makes a brand new name.

- *C* can easily be transformed into *G*.
  - And just a little ingenuity turns a lowercase *c* into a capital *Z*.

- *D* can be adjusted to a rather ugly *B*.

- But *E* can be transformed to an even better *B*.

- *F* can become a *P* or *R*.
    - It can also be changed into an *E*, which can then be made over into a *B*.

- A lowercase *h* can turn into a lowercase or capital *b/B*.
    - You can also make it a capital *H*, which probably won't help you all that much.

- *I* is awesome for you. It can be transformed into *B, D, E, F, H, K, L, M, N, P, R, T* or *W*... as in, WOW!

- A lowercase *j* can be adjusted to a very, very messy capital *S*.

- *L* can be adjusted to *D, E* or *I*.

- Only one stroke is needed to transform *N* into *M*.

- *O* can be made over into *Q*.
    - It can also become a really ugly D, or an even uglier B.

- Lowercase *o* can be turned into the number *8*. (good luck with that)

- *P* can become *B* or *R*. (cheap beer lovers will enjoy this one!)

- Capital *R* can only be transformed into a rough *B*.
  - However, lowercase *r* can turn into lowercase *m*, *n*, *o* or *p*.

- *S* can be adjusted to a horrifically ugly *Q*.

- *U* can become a not so great *V*, or an even worse *O*.
  - It can then be transformed into a pretty good *Q*.

- Finally, you don't need the best German engineering to make over a *V* into *W*.

o Perhaps your new letters still can't help you find a new name. Not to worry. Just find a new friend. There are over 300 million people in the United States and only Taylor Swift is friends with all of them. If you're too shy for being *Fearless*, you can also use your buddy's nickname. The best part is that you can always invent a new nickname, just like you can always invent more imaginary friends.

- *Nat* is now *Matthew*.
- *Perry* is now *Berry*.
- *Van* is now *Wanker*.
- *Fred* is now *Predator*.
- *Lance* is now *Dance Machine*.

- Okay, maybe in your case you can't change the name on the cover of the book. Not to worry… you still have options. If you are unable to use the name that's already on the blank line, just create a new blank line for yourself. This will require some minor arts and crafts. Pretend that it's your fake driver's license from high school and you won't have any problems.

  o Do you have any White Out or Liquid Paper around the house / apartment / motor home / yacht / dorm room / prison cell / jungle? Make sure that you shake the bottle first, before brushing the magical blunder eraser over the name that you wish to delete. (Since most of us do not have the hands of a surgeon, you may accidentally erase some of the actual blank line. If this happens, you can go back over it with a black pen to re-create the line on the page.) Give the liquid a few minutes to dry; listening to *November Rain* by Guns & Roses should give you more than enough time. Shake the book gently or blow on it a little. Once it's dry, you can write the new name onto your new blank line.

o You can also cover the old name with a blank label. This may not be as seamless as the previous suggestion, but it will take less time and artistic skill. You can find labels at your local office supply store. Do not remove the label from your mother's bottle of subscription pills, unless you are in fact giving this book to someone named Boniva. If one blank label is not strong enough to cover the original name, you can add a second label or even a third. There are about 30 labels to a sheet, so you will have plenty to work with if you make a mistake. Once the label is securely in place, you will once again be free to compose the new name.

o There's no rule that says you need to have a name on the front of the book. Instead of writing in a new name, try covering the old one with a sticker. There are many designs to choose from, depending on the mood you want to set with this show of generosity. Think of something that will make your lucky recipient smile… such as a rainbow, a butterfly, some balloons, a bunch of flowers or a pair of boobs.

- Still in doubt? Just give them this book without the cover. All of the important words will still be there to enjoy. Besides, plenty of writings have been successful without covers. The Magna Carta didn't have a cover. Neither did the Ten Commandments, which also succeeded without jokes... unless you count "thou shall not bear false witness against thy neighbor." Matthew McConaughey often fails to cover up, and he's a millionaire. So going without a cover does have its advantages.

- If you insist on pawning off your treasured book along with its cover, there is still one more risky trick you can try. Go out and buy the nicest wrapping paper you can find. I'll wait................... Just going to pour a glass of sherry here.......... Mmmm...... That's good sherry................. Oh look, you're back. I hope you don't mind that I finished the rest of the sherry while you were gone. Now, wrap the book tightly. Make sure that you place a large piece of tape directly over the name that you want to have removed. When your fortunate somebody removes the wrapping paper, they will also rip the cover in just the perfect spot. Not only will the hurtful evidence be erased, but as an added bonus you get to guilt them for damaging your gift!

• When all else fails, you can always go to the store and buy another copy of this book. Take the cover off the new book and place it on the old book; then take the cover off the old book and place it on your new book. Now you will have a clean cover to work with, plus you'll still have a copy of the book to keep for yourself. This makes everyone a winner. While you are not re-gifting your book anymore in the technical sense, this is still by far the finest option for you. And it's a sensational option for the person who gets your old gift, because they're getting the best present that's ever been invented on this or any other planet... a book!!!

But you already knew that, didn't you?

Also by the same author:

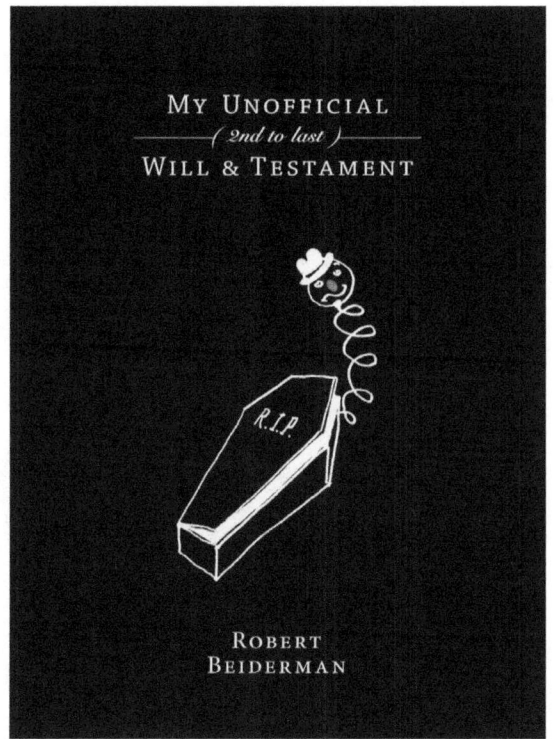

It's never too early to pay a man his final respects. This unofficial "legal" document will leave you in stitches while you learn how to properly dispose of the author's corpse, sit Shiva, and even build a proper shrine. (In return, you may be lucky enough to receive one of his earthly possessions.) A funny, original, and slightly ghoulish treat… reading this book is sure to be the time of your (after)life! ***My Unofficial (2nd to last) Will & Testament*** makes a perfect gift for deathbed confessions, mortician secret santas, nursing home housewarmings, and bat mitzvahs.

www.ingramcontent.com/pod-product-compliance
Lightning Source LLC
Chambersburg PA
CBHW071459070426
42452CB00041B/1933